50th Jubilee Immigration Anniversary from Ireland

HANDS ACROSS THE OCEAN

by

Prophetess Bridget White
Second Edition 2014

ISBN-13: 978-1-4993-0297-4

Poems ©2013-2014 Bridget White

Cover Illustration and interior black-and-white illustrations ©2013-2014 Colin Laing

All rights reserved. Without limiting the rights under copyright reserved above, no part of this publication may be reproduced, stored in a retrieval system, or transmitted, in any form or by any means (electronic, mechanical, photocopying, recording or otherwise), without the prior written permission of the copyright owner of this book.

BRISTOL UNDERGROUND PRESS

Introduction

All my family enjoyed roving through the green Irish hills. We would follow Mother, as she knew all the danger to look out for, such as rivers flowing with broken bridges laid out that could easily break. Cattle, not all of them friendly. It was there we

Me, recording on UCB Radio

would pick wild berries, sticks for the fire and mushrooms when they were out.

In the summer, we would go to Featherstone's land. There were many, many acres of lush green fields with rivers flowing through, and a big old mansion hidden away among tall trees that formed an avenue up the quarter of a mile or so. Mother often carried us on her shoulders when we were younger. She came from a small village called Raharny, a few miles from Caddagh, County Westmeath where we lived.

She did not feel at home with the people around there, and didn't form any friendships, which meant that she was very much alone after Father went to

England. They were different people from her. It took me years to see how unkind to her they all were.

Mother lost both parents when she was barely twenty years old. In those years Father was working in Kent in England, and he sent home the odd five pounds.

The rest of the time we had to beg, steal and borrow on a daily basis, but we were happy and contented with one another. Having such a good kind mother was a great start in life. She told us stories by candlelight. We had no electricity, radio or any comfort in our old cottage, but there was love and happiness.

We all had our liberty until Father came home, then the circus began. He went out to drink; he was a troubled man. There was no peace where he was, and I couldn't wait for him to go back to England.

One Easter he came into the church, drunk. He was carried out. I felt shame as Mother and I were there. He returned a few minutes later and stood up swaying from side to side, his black hair all tossed up. There was no one to help him or us. Here we were sitting in the big grand RC church in Delvin with the priest and altar boys looking so grand in their attire. The mission to save lost souls: where was it?

I was only a very young child, and inside I was crying for my poor mother who was doing all she could for us, my family sitting out in Caddagh in that old cold cottage with no food, yet here we were doing our Catholic duty sitting here listening to the Mass in Latin. I could not understand a word. We were looking up to the Pope in Rome and all the Catholic saints, but not all the rosary beads or medals could help us now. I despaired.

On one of my begging missions to get food I went to the priest's house and gave the housekeeper a little note asking for some food. As she opened the door I could smell a roast dinner. I handed her my note. A little later as I stood by the big polished door with its brass letter box and knocker, I heard the priest say, 'Who is it?' She said, 'It's Beasey White from Caddagh.' 'Well, tell her to come back next week'. What good would that be, I thought, when we are all starving now.

Old postcard of Delvin Church

I walked away. All the trees were green and the hedges well cut. The lawns looked lovely and green. My heart was heavy. How am I going to face my starving family now?

I looked high up in the sky at the steeple of this fine church. It was situated at the bottom of Delvin in its own grounds. Very grand indeed, but where is the mission I read about in books at school? The priests and nuns out in foreign fields, the reports that many of them were killed for their mission work ... then I heard these words: 'God is not here.' Then began my own mission: to find God.

I prayed for help. It came in the form of a few handfuls of flour and a bottle of milk. This was enough food to feed us for today. A farmer's wife; she gave me the widow's mite.

My school years were very troubled, mainly because I was mute at the time and couldn't get a word out. The teachers took this to be disobedience, often putting me in the dunce's corner, and on one occasion I was locked in a book cupboard and forgotten about. I had a view through a crack in the doors of the priest hearing first confession of girls who were preparing for their first Holy Communion.

One little seven-year-old girl was so full of fear of the priest, she flooded the floor. There she was kneeling in a puddle of her own urine, looking so dreadfully worried. Sin confessed she waddled away. Then the next girl came in and so on. I heard it all but it was much later when the teacher remembered to let me out. I tore up papers to occupy myself, and if it hadn't been for an opened window close to the cupboard I would not have been able to breathe.

This may sound like a story from the nineteenth century, but this was rural Ireland in the 1950s. I became a loner. The kids caught on to how the teachers were with me, and I was an outcast. I wanted to get involved with hopscotch and other games but it was always a no-no. 'Go away, White, we don't want you here.' Also I was left-handed, which was not accepted back then. My father was in England, so no father was an added plague. Not talking was not liked either, plus I was very poor and Mother struggled to get what lunch she could for us. But I just didn't come up to their expectations and I began to retaliate in my silence. I cut loose and made trouble for all my enemies. The fight was on.

Apart from a few kids from the Spike, a local poor row of houses outside Delvin – now these kids were poor but great – I would stand under a big old tree in Ballin Valley School yard and a few words would be exchanged. Suddenly my voice would utter a few words in the comfort of a few kids who were themselves the object of ridicule. There was scabies, head lice and poverty among these kids. Once my teacher, Miss. Carney told my mother in the village, 'The trouble with Beasey is that we can't keep her away from the lowly.' I was furious to hear this, as some of the other kids had ringworm and head lice too. Didn't we all at some time or another in our school days have these problems?

The one pound voucher Mother received from the Social didn't afford us much of a diet, not to mention our monthly family allowance which usually went to pay our rent on the old cottage.

Delvin at that time had some very affluent houses and occupants such as Dr Cox the vet, and the Merry Minstrel Show Band. One of them was Master Molloy who later taught me, and was a gentleman, and accepted me to do school work. I obliged.

The village held cattle fairs in which the village was taken over with cattle poo and slush and a bad smell. We used to walk through this mess on our way to school. My brothers often watched cattle for old farmers and earned a few shillings. Delvin had a good few pubs. The smell of stale beer and the yab of all the farmers plus the selling men and pots and pans made a funny old atmosphere in our village. It took weeks to rid the place of the smell, then back they came again.

This is a book of prophetic poems from my life, but soon I hope to write a book about my whole life, as there is so much more, but as a last bit of information about my poverty-stricken childhood in Ireland, I would like to say here that my mute condition did not get much better over the years. Right into my adult life I remained, in public, very quiet. But when I became a Christian in my early thirties I was encouraged to talk about my early childhood. It was then I began to get a lot more liberty because I had kept quiet about early childhood sexual abuse. I never talked about it.

Delvin

Just briefly, there were four men involved: a local neighbour, a man who worked for the local council who was involved with repairing our house, a young friend of Father's who later went to England, then the worst of all was to come. But I kept all this to myself and suffered abuse all through my life, even at school. There was no help, only ridicule for what they took for rebellion, which was really a cry for help. A cry that went unanswered. When I write my life story, then I can move on completely and leave all the rejection behind me, but it's only through the love of God and my mother and family that I am here to tell my story, as I so often contemplated a way out.

But if any of this happened to you, I beg you to seek help. Trust in God and you too will come though, I promise you. Don't feel alone. When you reach out for help you will meet good people who will help you through. As it says in the pages of the Holy book the Bible, love never fails.

Father took me out on three occasions and each time he lost me. When I was four he took me to church, but as we were walking down Delvin he swung me around and said, 'Do you want to go to high mass, low mass or no mass?' Then he proceeded to walk back up through the village again and into O'Shaughnessy's pub. There he bought me a small bottle of orange with a straw in it. He put me up on a big high stool. Then he disappeared down a dark room, where there was smoke and a terrible smell of stale beer.

I feared moving, as the stool was high and wobbly. There I sat for ages frozen in fear, until a small hunchback man came in to buy some food, as it was also a small grocery store. Seeing my predicament he offered to take me home and God bless him, he put me on the carrier of his bike and I had a dreadful time hanging on as he waddled from peddle to peddle. 'Keep your feet out and don't let go of that saddle. Hang tight.'

It was a mile and a half to Caddagh where he gently put me across the wall and said, 'run now into your house and see your mammy.'

I arrived home, and Mother was busy with her fourth baby, Charlie, who was just a few weeks old. She had no idea how I got back or of the ordeal that I had just been through.

On another occasion Father had abandoned me and my brother Sean who was eighteen months older than me, when we were three and four, at an event in our local hall. He said to one of the women,

'See they get home. I'm off to Delvin.'

On that occasion we were put into the hands of a local youth called Paddy Anderson. He was not going to get us home before he'd had some blaggard fun at our cost. He took us across the fields and threatened to throw us both into the river. We were scared, but he did eventually drop us home.

Another time Father took me to a gymkhana in the fields of Clunnan Castle in Delvin and left me with a handful of ice-cream and bottles of orange. He said, 'Sit there and I will be back with the others in a minute.'

The sun belted down and the ice-cream began to melt. I ate all the ice-cream and drank all the orange. He didn't come back so there I sat in the sweltering sun, sick and scorched, until eventually I was found and brought home. The doctor was called and that was the last time Father ever brought me out again. He was totally on his own trip, living in his own world — which was his boys as he called them, the pub. He was not capable of looking after himself as he often got drunk and was carried home by one of the boys or some other person who had a heart to do so. He was a broken man, medicating himself with beer to get through his emotional weakness and his inner turmoil.

Father went to England because he had burned all his boats. He simply called my older brother aside and said, 'Do what your mother asks of you as she won't ask you to do anything wrong. I'm not man enough for the job. No, I'm going to England to work, so you look after things here.'

He never looked at me as I stood there with tears welling up and a lump in my throat. I went to the back garden and said to myself, 'I will not cry. I will not cry.' From that day on I became tough; I had to survive in a fatherless world. The feeling of total rejection and abandonment on a small child almost killed me. Little did I know the damage this would do to me. I could help people by doing jobs but emotionally I was cut off from Mother and all my family. I was like a robot, locked up, hurt and untrustful, damaged beyond all things, and I loved Jesus and I never stopped knowing He loved me.

I found the strength to go on, and I did have a great love for my mother and brothers and sisters, and I worried a great deal about them. I always kept them all closely in my prayers at night as I still do today, and all my family. God is my refuge and a great help in times of trouble. To Him be all the glory.

Mary Grant (right) with me, her bridesmaid

My poems are based on my life and heartaches, when no one loves you or understands you. Then God is there. He is not contained in a big building. He doesn't speak Latin. In fact, He came down to live among us in Israel among the Jews. He is Jesus; Father, Son and Holy Spirit, all One.

No greater love than this, He laid down His life for us all to pay our transgressions. He was pierced, hung on the cross. Our disobedience, our wanting to go our own way to a miry pit, but still He holds out a hand of restoration to us all. 'Come follow Me and I will make you a fisher of men' – the Great Commission. He holds the key. He will redeem you, restore you to Himself. All you have to do is repent.

We all emigrated to England in the mid-sixties. Father sobered up long enough to get us out of Ireland, just as the troubles were brewing up in the North. He was motivated by letters he received from Ireland asking him to remove me from the O'Higgins family in Dalkey: Mr TF O'Higgins was running for the Presidency – I was a nanny who was living fulltime in their Dalkey home looking after their seven children. The IRA were rising up to fight for a United Ireland, and did not want a member of the O'Higgins family as President. They had killed a few members of his family already in previous years. Father was of the same mind; he secured an IRA safe house in Bristol and took us all out of Ireland.

Michael, my eldest

The landlord was a Belfast man. I spent two years living in and working with the RC nuns in St Mary's Hospital, Clifton where no one knew why we had left Ireland. Two more children came along – a sister and a brother. Now there were nine of us. Father returned to Kent and set up his life where he left off. We were now deserted in Bristol. We knew no one.

I have three children. But life was up and down. I have worked among the homeless in the Salvation

Army and later went on to run, with Simon, a drop-in for homeless people, getting some off the street. I became homeless myself and was stripped of all my worldly possessions, but that's another story.

I have six very wonderful grandchildren, but not without more pain, as I continue to try to build up my life again. I come from a big, close Irish family but that comes with lots of baggage also, though we have all at times helped each other. However only God is the One who makes the difference.

My family have, like every other family, been rocked by events but never more so than when my nephew lost his little daughter, Olivia.

That left a big, big gap, and it was and still is hard to know how that young man coped with such sorrow – only by God's grace.

I dedicate this book to:

My mother Catherine who was always there for me. Thanks so very much,

To my six brothers and two sisters,

To my three precious children,

And equally precious grandchildren, all six of them,

To the people who believed in me as a person,

My friend Jackie,

But a big, big thank you to Simon Farris. We met at the time the drop-in for the homeless started at the Elmgrove Centre in Bristol, and for the last twelve years we have travelled and evangelised all over the place, and done a mini mission to Delvin. We have worked on the streets of Bristol, going from skateboard parks to McDonalds to reach the kids for God.

Thousands have believed in Jesus through this outreach. We have done radio and have lots on YouTube. We are often called in to counsel people. Simon has been a very good friend and has made such a difference to my life. Simon not only encour-

After baptising George (front)

aged me to publicise my poems, but he has done all the typing, enduring but never complaining, but always encouraging me. He is a very brave man to have done all this, and for that I am eternally grateful. Thanks, Simon.

P.S. I thank my sister Mary. She, by God's grace, helped to save my life in the early '70s, when I suffered a miscarriage. I arrived in hospital with very little time to spare due to blood loss. She was only 16 years old. She also looked after my son who was only 18 months old at the time.

The proceeds from this book will go to help the homeless, whoever they are,
  Also to the Olivia White fund for cancer, in memory of my great-niece, to buy machines at the

Children's Hospital at the BRI Bristol.

Grateful thanks also goes to Colin Laing, my brother-in-law, who drew and gave me the front cover and the illustrations inside. He may be contacted on colinlaing580@hotmail.co.uk

My contact details are:

Bridget White
c/o The Garden Flat
61 Springfield Road
Cotham
Bristol
BS6 5SW
England

Email: bristolundergroundchurch@yahoo.co.uk
YouTube: Simonbridget
Telephone: 07506 916 479 and 07773 062 980

Thanks very much also to Chris Wright, provided by a miracle, my editor who volunteered his services, who is also a friend of Simon and me.

My father, Tom White, played hurling for Co. Westmeath, and in 1953 his team won. He was also a keen cricketer, and was mentioned a few times in the local paper. The paper ran a photograph of him and his full team in 1953.

I am hoping to tell my life story soon in more detail, in a book called *The Shirtwhite's Daughter*.

God gave me these verses for this book:

> **8** But ye, O mountains of Israel, ye shall shoot forth your branches, and yield your fruit to my people of Israel; for they are at hand to come.
> **9** For, behold, I am for you, and I will turn unto you, and ye shall be tilled and sown:
> **10** And I will multiply men upon you, all the house of Israel, even all of it: and the cities shall be inhabited, and the wastes shall be builded:
> **11** And I will multiply upon you man and beast; and they shall increase and bring fruit: and I will settle you after your old estates, and will do better unto you than at your beginnings: and ye shall know that I am the Lord.
> **12** Yea, I will cause men to walk upon you, even my people Israel; and they shall possess thee, and thou shalt be their inheritance, and thou shalt no more henceforth bereave them of men (Ezekiel 36:8-12).

I am looking for a composer to put music to my first poem. I heard it being sung in my dream. If you are interested, please contact me.

Poems by page number

1	Such love from on high
2	A love divine
3	When men live a lie
5	Saved at the cross
9	He holds the key
12	What God can do
13	Take Exit 7
15	Jesus Christ
18	Shepherd boy
19	God cares
21	In the absence of God, man will fall
23	Walk with Jesus

IRELAND

27	No more fireside talk- prophecy for Ireland
30	A long way from home out all alone
33	Childhood abuse
35	Gerry Ryan
39	Irish immigrant
41	Big Tom
44	Hands across the ocean
47	The Celtic Tiger
50	Childhood
53	Tom
54	Old Mrs Fagin
56	Mr White
59	The Irish hills
62	The Wimpey boy
65	In old Delvin
67	A begging letter from an Irish mother
70	Ireland
72	Ballin Valley

75   Poverty lurks
78   Don't waste another day
79   Once a lowly beggar
83   Broken kid

GANGSTER
88   Wild Goose
90   The black Flash
94   The prisoner
98   Tiny Feet
101 Wouldn't walk the line
104 The hooded guy with the darkened eye
107 The dope's got the bloke
109 The petition
114 The cop's got the gun
117 The bounty hunter
120 Wacky backy
123 Bring back the kids

SPECIFIC TOPICS
127 Mother dear
129 Greetings my fair ones
130 Walk
132 Dreams
134 Don't play games
136 Days gone bye
137 How do you know?
139 Revival India
141 Winter
143 Foster and adopt
145 Being troubled
148 For Sandra in the '90s
150 Fault
151 Frost
155 That's all

157	Riverside
158	Osama Bin Laden
160	10, Downing Street
163	9/11 USA- Echoes of broken glass
166	Amy Winehouse
169	Tsunami
171	Immigration
173	Volcano
176	March 2011
178	William and Kate's wedding date
181	Our Queen
183	Chains
185	Time
187	Mountain high
188	My steps are built on heartache
190	Japan, Japan, Japan
193	War, war, war
195	I would rather
197	Give up smoking
199	Memories
201	2013
203	The summer rose
205	Winter winds
206	Time holds no place
207	Crying in the wilderness
208	The moon looked on
211	At night
214	The fall-away
215	In vain
217	Autumn
218	Rest my case
222	Bella dear
223	Barack Obama

Such Love From On High

Worldly love will come and go
As surely as the oceans waters flow;
It will have its ups and downs,
Turn you up and twist you all around.
This love is not very strong
And more often it doesn't last very long;
It takes you to a height
And then drops you like a deflated kite.

But the love I have just for you
Is gently meekly flowing true,
As naturally as the oceans waters do.
It comes down from on high;
It's truthful and without a lie,
It cares for you when you are here or there,
It always remembers and never forgets
And nothing, in return, it expects;
It lasts for ever and a day,
Whether here or there.

It watches you from afar and near,
It's without jealousy or fear;
It sees your inner hurt and pain
And wants to comfort you time and time again.
It sees your inner conflict and emotions
That are so deep; deep as the oceans
Where an earthly love cannot reach
And only love from on high can teach.
Where did I find such love just for you,
That is so humble and true?

It's a gift from God, not for me, but for you,
And in return you would see His love just for you.

A Love Divine

I reached your gentle heart
With a flow of tears that kept us apart,
I did not want to sin and die.
Knowing to my Saviour I could not die,
The ways of this world would have taken us wrong,
In the end my faith was too strong.
I watched your gentle smile
That lasted for a short while.
I know some things you didn't understand.
Both of us in the end God wanted to defend.
You were like a long-lost friend
Whose needs I had to attend,
I loved your gentle ways
When I spent with you all these days.
You were so meek and mild,
Just like a long lost child
Who I found on my lonely way;

So I am grateful to God every day
For the time we spent together
Just like birds of one feather.
We assembled on the ancient road,
Both of us carrying our load;
You need a wing to shelter you,
Just like all God's children do.
God worked in mysterious ways
When we were together all these days;
He wanted to know you more clearly,
So that you could love Him more dearly;
I asked God to forgive me every day
For how my own feelings got in the way.
Then God showed me His love for you.
It was a love divine,
Which left my love for you far behind.

When Men Live a Lie

When men live a lie,
Watch them die by and by,
When for the truth they cannot cry.
Watch God pass them by and by,
They would sooner have their shame,
Carry all the blame,
Be lost and die in the flame.

They say hell does not exist,
In anger hold up their fists;
They do not thirst, but put themselves first,
For the will of God would bring them reward.
They prefer to be lost than turn to the Cross
Where their Redeemer lives.
For them His life He gives;

Why do men run and hide?
The World is big and wide,
They need to bend a knee,
Then they could be free,
Not depend on themselves.
Put God's favours on a shelf,

Man thinks he knows it all,
Disobeys God's call,
Now watch him fall.
He has got no hope at all,
Unless he turns around
He will be lost and not found.

Jesus knows their every sorrow,
He holds their tomorrows,
So why delay? Everything's not ok.
You will surely fall

If you refuse Gods call;
Leave down all your pain,
There's a lot to gain;
Your life will not be in vain.
You will be your own worst enemy,
Never to be free;
You cannot forgive your own sins,
You are not able your Salvation to win.

Jesus is your only hope,
Eternity you cannot elope;
You must face the judgement seat,
Avoid hell's heat.
What do you think?
Can you make the link?
Without Jesus you will sink.

Your salvation He has won,
Now all your sins are gone
If you accept He has won:
Otherwise you are lost.
Your life without God in eternity
Is your greatest loss.

A Christmas party at The Shepherd's Tent

Saved at the Cross

Saved at the Cross – now my family are not lost;
Get down on your knees, take every need,
Jesus will meet you there;
He is gentle and fair,
He died for your cares,
No need to carry your load;
He is the narrow road,

Do not despair,
Leave every sin there.
You cannot do it on your own,
You are not alone;
His love will carry you there,
You will find He really does care.
Come, listen, obey,
Don't dither and delay;
Jesus is here to stay.
Don't any longer go astray,
Turning your back on the only One,
Your case He has already won.

After all, He is the Fathers Son:
The Father, Son and Holy Ghost,
They are the Ones that love you the most.
Why waste another day?
Come now, don't delay,
It's your holy Father's day:
He is reaching out with loving arms,
Come now, don't be alarmed,
You're the apple of His eye.
He wants you now, not by-and-by;
He is the God of the living, don't you know?
Don't no longer hang low,
He paid the price on the cross,
Paving the way for the lost:
Yes, that's right, you are lost.

Lay down your empty pride,
Come and reside, do not run and hide.
He knows your every sin and sorrow,
He will give you a better tomorrow.
Don't look at other peoples short-comings,
Forsaking your own livings;
Jesus is looking at you,
Hoping you will be true;
Give your whole life over to Him,
Stop being out on a limb.
Now come and confess all your sins to Him:
On your own, you can't win.
Surely you know that by now
Jesus has all the power;
You can't do it on your own,
Trying to live your life all on your own.

By now you should have seen the light:
Jesus loves you by day and by night.

What are you hanging on to?
That's no good for you;
Forgive those who offended you,
Then your sins are forgiven too.
You do not have the answers to all your cares.
So come to Jesus and leave them all there.
Don't carry them through another day,
Come and get your Salvation, now today.
Don't dither and delay
Or sit on the fence another day
Licking your wounds; they won't go away.

It's Jesus who paid the price,
Basically you have no other choice:
But hell is a dreadful option.
You know it makes sense not to sit on the fence
Ignoring Jesus and what He went through for you.
Don't look at other people's sin,
Put yours in the waste bin,
Move on to a better life
Without damnation and strife.
Come on, you only got one life,

Why hold yourself in prison
And throw away the key?
Don't be angry or afraid,
Jesus his life down he laid;
Come today and be with Him, not out on a limb;
Choose life, not death – which is an option.
But surely you will make the right choice,
It will settle your Eternal destiny.
Make it clear which side you are on
For there is a battle going on, for your soul.
Jesus has already won.

Which side are you on?
You can't string God along,
He knows the beginning and the end;
Don't be a fool, but be wise – make the right choice
Because the option is not very nice.
Hell fire is burning,
But Jesus love is yearning,
And burning, his light is so bright,
His love is so right.
How could you choose wrong?
His light is so bright,
His love is so right,
How could you choose wrong?
You may have done that for too long,
Knowing that it's all wrong;

Don't be a fool, go through life with no tools,
Jesus has it all – now make that call.
PLEASE, Jesus, forgive me all my sins
That I have committed in my lifetime.
I have repented of them,
And accept that you have forgiven me fully,
And that I have Eternal life.
Now be baptised by full immersion.
Now you are born again.
Jesus is the Saviour of the whole world.
Why stay lost,
When you can bring it all to Jesus
at the CROSS?

He Holds the Key

I've got my visa,
I can enter in;
Heaven is my home,
I am not alone,
He holds the key,
I've got my visa,
I can enter in.
He paid the price,
He is the Christ,
He holds the key,
I've got my visa,
I can enter in.
He took my sins,
Then He let me in;
He holds the key,
I've got my visa,
I can enter in.
He holds my sorrows
and all my tomorrows;
He holds the key,

I've got my visa,
I can enter in.
I have repented,
He has relented;
He holds the key,
I've got my visa,
I can enter in.
He is my Judge
and my Jury;
He holds the key,
I've got my visa,
I can enter in.
He took to the cross,
His life He lost;
He holds the key,
I've got my visa,
I can enter in.
He gave me His love
When He came from above;
He holds the key.
I've got my visa,
I can enter in.
I have been forgiven,
Now I am living;
He holds the key,
I've got my visa,
I can enter in.
I have been healed,
Now I can really feel.
He holds the key,
I've got my visa,
I can enter in.
His love for me
Is making me free;
He holds the key,

I've got my visa,
I can enter in –
His truth is rolling through –
And so can you.
He holds the key,
I've got my visa,
I can enter in.
His Name is Jesus Christ,
He paid the price;
He holds the key,
I've got my visa,
I can enter in.
Eternal life He did win,
Now *you* can enter in;
He holds the key.
Have you got your visa?
Can you enter in?
Lay down your sin,
Repent, come on in,
He holds the key.
You've got your visa:
Come on in,
Be baptized,
To new life arise.
He holds the key:
Here's your visa,
COME ON IN.

What God Can Do

What God can do
If hearts go astray;
It knows not the way
If it is left on its own;
It knows not the way home.

Yet God with all His strength
And power
Can descend and melt
Your heart like a little flower.

Simon and I preaching at a meeting we held
for the homeless in 2012

Take Exit 7

We went to London last week
Some excitement to seek,.
And what we found in the Underground
Were some men, tired, lonely and weak;

The whole place was alive,
But down under, what a dive,
With the lowly trying to survive
In a fast flowing city,
No time for pity.

For God's people are alive,
The opportunity is fast moving by;
Not a sign of the church in sight.
Where did they run and hide?
Not wanting God's people to be alive,
Put aside by the fast flowing life;
And come outside, for surely God's people are alive.

Don't hide away like the world today,
Letting men fade away
To a world they have no say.
They are just children, getting in the way
Of a fast moving world today;
It's not God's plan to ignore
The needy and poor
For He has given you so much more.

Please, Church, you battle within;
Lay down your weapons of war,
It's all gone too far,
For the cardboard city it's just an eye-sore
And a pity.
As people rush on by, the just sigh,

And looking to the ground, not searching in their heart
The desperation of these people in the Underground.

For I came away feeling different inside;
Those emotions I cannot hide,
God's people are really alive.
Wake up, Church, don't run and hide,
For those people are outside,
And tears from heaven are falling down
To God's people in the Underground;
Flooding this place with unrest.
You have got the tools – God rules.

Oh, know they are not fools,
Just children waiting in the Underground.
O people of God, hidden inside church walls,
How long will you be in prison?
Don't you know, you are in possession of keys
Those people to release?

It only takes a little faith
To open the door – and in heaven, listen to the roar.
God's people must not hold in store, God's provisions,
But to release those lowly waiting in the Underground.

They are in prison outside,
You are in prison inside,
But the truth will set you free.
Prison is not the place God wants either,
Of you to dwell in a dying cell.
Just because man fell.
Jesus has paid the price:
Jesus is the way, the truth and the life.

Jesus Christ

Why the search
For what does not exist?
Every person's itch.
They look everywhere
But don't find it there.

A man may find a wife
That will last him all his life;
A woman may find a man
That will do all he can

And still not understand
Why the searching goes on
And on and on far beyond.

The sun may shine
And in that they find
It doesn't bring peace of mind;
The rainy day will come,
Then out will come the sun.

Still they all run,
Searching for some fun;
The snow brings its show,
No school, kids go out slow.

Only GOD can fill that empty place;
Hand it over, give up the chase.
Only in Him will you find peace of mind,
All that is loving and kind.

Give up all your sorrows,
Give God all your tomorrows,
For He is the missing piece
That will release
All the heartache that is bound up.

Teach you to wait and stop,
But above all, don't give up,
God is all you need;
Life will now be sweet,
Accept His teaching,
Go out reaching
To spread His word:
That is very good.
Your searching days are over,

You have got God's cover;
Get up with the lark,
Go preaching in the park.

The night was dark,
Now God's light has shone,
Your soul He has won;
He paid the price:
HE IS JESUS CHRIST.

Shepherd Boy

Can you hear the call of the Shepherd boy?
He's ringing out a call to you and I.
Can you hear the sound, it's ringing all around?
It's a call to come close
To the one you love the most:
The Father, Son and Holy Ghost.
Hear the call it's loud and clear,
Can you hear, it's coming near?
Step out and do not fear,
The Shepherd boy is ringing loud and clear.
Can you hear the call of the shepherd boy?
He's ringing out for you and I.
Now draw very close, to the Father, Son and Holy Ghost:
Let them be the One you love the most.

Evangelizing in Easton, Bristol

God Cares

The sun always settled
And came to a close
At the foot of the garden
Where I hung out my clothes.

Then I knew that it was
Time to go indoors
And the sky would
Soon be full of stars.

As I lay down my head
The moon was afire;
It shone its light through
The bedroom door
That was ajar.

Then my thoughts would stray
Through the troubles of my day;
I would wring the good from the bad,
What made me sad or glad.

Then I had to get out of bed
And tell Jesus my sorrows
And pray for better tomorrows,
For I know that He cares.

He bears my burdens,
Now I have peace to close
my eyes
And picture the sky,

Knowing that my Heavenly Father
Is taking care,
Not just up there,
But also down here.

In the Absence of God, Man Will Fall

In the days of old,
The youth were told,
"Behave, be good, don't be bold."
They took advice,
Were ever so nice.

It took the whole community to bring them up;
If they misbehaved, they were told to stop
By the butcher, the baker or local cop.

Everyone kept a look-out
For the local lout,
If he didn't behave, he was kicked out.

Now the Church played a great big part,
Putting them on the right road from the start;
For the youth and kids, they had a heart.

Read the word of God,
It will put you on the right road.
Now time has long past,
Youth have grown up too fast;
No one seems to care too much.
Parents and teachers are out of touch,
Gone is the butcher, baker and local cop.
If you tell them to stop
You'll get locked up.

With all the human rights
The streets are full of violence and fights.
Drugs have taken the place of hugs;
Love and compassion
have gone out of fashion.

Kids get too much wrong things,
Their senses have flown away on wings,
Wasting time playing on TV and games
Making their young minds very lame.
There's not much hope,
Taking all that dope
Filling up all their veins,
Wasting all their brains.

They deny themselves no vain things,
Some even call themselves street-kings.
Why do they cry, "We'll die"?
Why?

Giving out gospel tracts
in the Muslim community

Walk With Jesus

Me, at King's College, Cambridge

With Jesus walk, I will.
He will take all my cares away
If I walk with Him today,
I do not have to fear
What I cannot see;
With Him all day, I long to be.

All His ways are free,
He died for you and me.
Gave up all He had, here
So we'd all be free up there
In heaven's green air.

Where He promises we won't have a care,
And love will be all around;

All the rest will not be found.
So whatever you are carrying today,
Lay it down and walk this way.

You have a Saviour that really cares,
He is totally fair,
You can trust Him all the time.
This, if you follow him, you will find
He is always loving and kind.

He requires one thing of you:
Obey His word,
Read the word today.
In the Bible written in red
Follow this; you will be fed, led
To His kingdom. It has no end.
Why would you ignore
To your own sore?

All that He offers you,
It cost you nothing. Don't rue,
And lose out, whatever you do.
Beyond this, there is nothing.
All will be ill-gotten,
And you will only ever be
Left carrying the wrapper
Instead of enjoying His provision.

What's your final decision?
With Jesus, let there be no division.
It will cost you the loss of your soul
As, into heaven, all the rest will roll.
Don't be left outside like a fool;
In heaven and earth, follow God's rule.

God can't change His mind
To accommodate you being left behind;
It would purely be your decision
To allow this division.

It's heaven or hell:
Where will you for eternity dwell?
Turn your back on His plan?
You will never get the chance again.
In heaven you will continue to live,
Because Jesus, you he has forgive.

All your sins are washed away
By the blood He shed that day.

Hell is a burning fire
For the lost sinner and liar.

Heaven is awaiting,
You must not be hesitating;
Jesus loves you, come on in,
Abandon all your sin.
Jesus paid the price
Once for all.

Can you hear the call?
Abandon all,
Come, on your knees fall.
God will hear that call.

IRELAND

No More Fireside Talk — Prophecy for Ireland

Oh you cruel and troubled Land, look at all the casualties you have spat out,
It's not even the overflow.
I will not worship you, or give any glory to you;
You are not free
You are in bondage
Surrounded by every false idol and idolatrous land, covered by the blood of pagans and idolatry. Your people are perishing.
You have been gate-crashed by far and near; you live in constant fear, a hell on earth.
What do you promise your people?
An eternal hell.
What do you ask of them?
Glory for yourself; idolatry with all your falsehood, to stay in ignorance,
To be blinded to all your ways.
You have got millions of questions but few answers, if any at all.

But listen, hear, lend an ear, cast aside all your fears. Can I engage your thoughts? Have I got your attention? Have I got your understanding? Is your heart listening? Can your mind cast out wrong thoughts? Can it tell right from wrong? Is there mercy in your heart? Will you not listen with a condemning heart to what I say?

Have you taken in generations of fireside talk? Did you give that your attention? Did you listen to stories of long, long ago about people you didn't know, and judge them on the strength of what the speaker said about things that did happen in their fathers' day? And in your mind did you set up a judge and jury to execute, loot, or imprison those you found guilty? When are you going to set them free? Has any of this dawned on you and, when your day is done, will you hand those keys down to your children to continue building your prison of souls you have kept hidden from long, long ago? Do you feel the need to continue doing this fireside talk?

If so, my dear lost friend, listen to what I say. Lend me your ear; pay attention to what I say. Hear, child, come away from that fire. One day it's going to BURN you eternally, along with all you quote daily by its side. And hear some living WORDS; yes, real living WORDS that will save you from that fire and lead you on the narrow road where your SAVIOUR is waiting. But first, my dear lost friend, you need to do something. First, admit you are wrong, then repent of the wrong. Now ask God to forgive you; then know you are forgiven: now the journey begins.

Now God can reason with you. Let go of everything you know. If it's rebellion then it will have to go. If it's anger, or bitterness, then it will have to go.

You are now called out to be separated from the world though still living in it. If it's rejection, or jealousy it will have to go in the name of JESUS. You will now have to claim your freedom. You are on the way to becoming a new creation.

Those chains will be broken by God. He will release you a little at a time. Your wounds will be healed – Isaiah 53. Your broken heart will be replaced by a heart of flesh. You will have a new spirit and your mind will be renewed. God will give you back the years the locust has eaten. He will guide, protect, prepare – Psalm 23. He will shelter you – Psalm 91.

And at the end of all this He will prepare an eternal place for you with HIM. It's a **trip of a lifetime**, because it never ends:

And it costs you nothing. NO, because JESUS died on the cross.
He paid in full
IT IS DONE
NO MORE FIRESIDE TALK.

Back left to right: Ann Doyle, Johnny Devine, William Doyle, (my cousins) and me. Front: Sean (my brother).

A Long Way From Home Out All Alone

I wander through the streets
Hoping someone to meet;
My heart is heavy and beat
Above the summer heat.
The air is sweet,
People rush by; no "Hi,"
I give a deep sigh;
"See you by and by."

I stroll through country lanes
They all seem the same;
There the sound of flowing water,
Our hearts remember
That it's now September,
School time is here,
A burden I must bear.
I am only twelve years old,
Out in the Autumn cold.

The summer is here,
I am older by one year;
No father here, I am lonely,
No one to love me only.
I now have to work
To help feed the family,
But this I do with love,
It came down from above;
It was a heavy year
That I had to bear;
I know God's love up there,
I hand Him my Burdens and Cares

The winter winds are blowing,
Outside it's snowing;
The robin is hopping about,
I can't go out.
Our old house is very cold
No heat, my brothers are bold;
The sticks on the fire are hissing,
The kettle won't boil; I am hissing.
There's no running water or heat,
I feel sad and beat.
I fetch some water from the iced pond
Over in the field beyond.

There's no bread in the house,
We haven't eaten for three days.
If we are to live I will have to beg.
Up the icy road I go, it's a mile or more,
Then I knock on the door.
Can I have some milk and bread?
The lady looks sad, so does the farm lad.
She hands me a small supply. Off I fly.
Back at the old house the fire is dim,
No kettle on the brim, mother is feeling grim.
I put bread and milk on the table;
After a little food the day to face we will be able.

What will tomorrow bring?
It's winter, so the birds won't sing;
It will be back out to beg, steal and borrow,
It's a heavy load for a little child with sorrow.
Father sent no money from England again,
And Oh what a lot of pain.
He has been drinking and living wild,
And forgotten mother and child:
We are living in a forgotten land.

We pray God will lend a helping hand;
Every day we survive and stay alive.
Where are our justices?
Where is our love?
Who cares?
Who?
Only God Our Father in heaven.
He is my justice, He loves, He cares there,
And He does all this for you. Praise Him. Give Him glory.
He cared when I didn't have a crust of bread,
He didn't let me die:
So to Him be all the glory on high.

Me, aged 19

Childhood abuse

Were you too proud?
Your actions spoke out loud.
You denied me as a child,
Preferring instead to go out wild.
You got all dressed up,
Didn't know where to stop.

All through my childhood years
And my blocked up tears
I wasn't allowed to speak
For fear your actions would leak.

I was controlled,
Kept within the fold.
'Put your best foot forward,
Shake off the dust.
Put a good show on you must',
Was the order of the day.

My growth delayed,
But inside locked up
I had to hide.
All my feelings
Came in like a rushing tide.

Bringing in all
The broken fragments of my life.
Then dragged back out
To a roaring sea
Where they lay still
Until the next tide.

It's time to pick up the pieces
With all its releases.
Come, let me talk,
Then all my broken dreams will walk
And with them I will never meet again.

Me with my brother Tom in Bristol
in the late 1960s

Gerry Ryan

Said Yes every time
To the white dust
That became a must;
For a time it lifted him up.
What vile stuff
Brought over to Ireland
By those who offend.

He was hooked
By the very crook;
How many more
On Ireland's green shore
Will drop down like a fly
And die?

All because they wanted a high,
Poor Gerry, even at his age
Paid such a wage;
His life stopped at this page.

Cocaine brought in all this pain.
Tomorrow they will be here again,
Selling the white stuff
That in the end will make you feel rough.

Many will die seeking
This high.
The crooks got rich;
Our men die in the ditch.

Who can stop these drugs?
Who can hold back the toughs?
Where the shamrock grows

They have spilt the po
Bringing our land so low
Far across the ocean
Where the vile stuff grows.

Who can stop it now, how?
It will claim more lives,
Leaving child and wives;
It's an evil weed
That brings in a bad seed
Where the man of greed,
AN ADDICT to feed.

God's anger will surely fall
When He hears my call:
Get them out of there,
Out of our land so small,
Don't let them carry their poison
At every sun rising.

People are getting hooked,
Their destiny booked;
What a plight.
Come on, kick up a fight,
Don't let this dark night
Keep the light out of sight.

Stand together
In the land of heather;
Pray to God to get free,
Or in slavery forever be.

For the white stuff has arrived
With evil on its side;
Shout and kick it out,

For men will die
And cry.

It's a foreign weapon,
With no gun
To fire the powder cocaine.

Irish Immigrant

I am an Irish immigrant,
By God I was sent
To a land full of sin,
Their souls for God to win.
Over forty years I spent
Hoping, from their sins, they would relent.

Bristol has been my home,
From it I do not want to roam;
This has been a mission,
For saving souls I go fishing.

I know God is well worth knowing,
That's where everything is going;
Nothing else is worth doing
Or pursuing.

I want to follow Him;
In the world the light is dim,
Jesus is the Light,
Keep Him in your sight,
For you He fought the good fight:
He won,
He is God's only Son.

For you He died on the cross,
Took all your loss;
Follow Him
Where the light is not dim.
Come on in,
Your soul He did win,

Taken away all your sin;
You will bear fruit
That the enemy cannot loot.

For if you follow this way
Your life will be good every day.
Jesus loves you
(What will you do?)
The door is open, come on in,
Pack in all your sin;
Repent from time spent
Sinning wherever you went.

Big Tom

Tom White (my father)

Lonely I walk
Without a friend to talk,
Far away from home
And all alone;
I am only a man,
I will do the best I can:
My wife and children in another land.

I am looking for work on a distant shore,
But right now I am feeling very low.
Mother passed away when I was four,
Left me on the cold, cold floor.
My Daddy was a crippled man
In more ways than one he didn't understand.

He held on to his money,
Fed me on wild honey.
Friends and neighbours I had but few.
Often I was feeling lonely and blue.

God gave me a great wife.
I was made up for life.
Then followed my children-
All asleep in the pen.

I was a wild young man,
Life I didn't understand.
I drank too much,
Left my wife in the lurch.
Followed some lonely days,
Mixed up wild ways.

Now to work I have come,
To England without a crumb;
I walk the lonely street
With tired feet.

Thinking about my wife and kids back home,
Wishing for work – I hadn't to roam.
A man can lose his way
When with his wife he won't stay,
When at other women he starts to stare.

He can easily go astray;
He sees things through rose-coloured glasses,
Make his life turn into ashes.
Where once there were blooming roses.

The man with ignorant causes
Ties his life up with knots and crosses,

Never winning but is losing.
Too much boozing and snoozing,
The man's lost the plot,
His life he brought to naught,
And tied everything up in knots.

Only God can release.
Bring him a bit of peace;
Became a complete fool,
Not keeping God's rule.

He brought others astray,
All losing the way;
None could find their way home,
Now they are out there alone.

To leave the way
Brought a hopeless day,
The miles that kept us apart;
The long lonely nights with a broken heart,
Too many years have passed,
I can see sense at last
But I am caught up in the past.

Married another wife:
The biggest mistake of my life;
Spent too much time in the pub
With the boys.
Sure it was the devil's work
In disguise.
Too late.
By God's grace
I am wise.

Hands Across the Ocean

We travelled that night
Until the hills of Ireland
Were out of sight,
And for a small fee
We crossed the Irish sea.
It was the old mail boat
That kept us afloat;

The year was 1964
When we came knocking on England's door.
It was after the Second World War,
These shores had been broken
To their core.
We came into the old station:
What a crowd,

The loud speakers were loud,
The train pulled away,
Now we were here to stay.

We grabbed a cab
And spent all we had;
The house was small,
I don't know how we
All fitted in at all.

We left a house and acre,
Which was sold to the first taker.
Now we had burnt
All our boats.
Stay here we ought,

Life had its ups and downs;
Left behind was the Irish pound,
And in its place
The Queen's face.
We all had to earn our living,
Back to a new society we were giving,
And, by God's grace,
We joined in this race.
We had to forgive them
When they didn't want us
To live with them.
No dogs, no Irish, no blacks.

But now, looking back
This was England
In 1964
When prejudice came
Knocking on our door.
We had the stamp of immigration,

They had the nerve of temptation,
But still we lingered on
Until most of that was gone.
But through the years
And the unspilt tears
Gives us a break,
We haven't come to take
But to work, to share,
To live and care.

We have reached out a hand
Across the Irish sea,
So please, let us be
And wander free.
I am still Irish, don't you see
And you have taken such good care of me.

The Celtic Tiger

The Celtic Tiger was out
Of sight
When we left Ireland
That night,
As we sailed away
To a bright new day.

Upon a foreign shore
We would explore;
Gone would be the poverty
And in its place the sovereignty;
And under the British Crown
We would settle in another town,
And in the coming years
Ireland done well,
And the Northern fighting fell.

They all got rich;
No more digging poreens out
Of the ditch.
They too became proud,
And in came the foreign crowd.
They built new houses and roads,
The immigrant went off carrying their loads
To foreign fields like goats.
Back home we got good reports:

"Stay where ye are,
We are going far;
The Euro is the way to go,
Because you haven't got it
You are slow.
We can hardly keep up.
We are so near the top."

Every letter full of delight,
We have almost reached our height;
The streets of England are not paved with gold.
Watch what you are told.
The Celtic Tiger had run
Through Ireland's land.
(It was get all you can.)

But everyone has his day
And sure, it wasn't here to stay;
In a matter of time
It began to decline.

Some took their own lives,
Left behind kids and wives.
The golden age
Recorded on this page.

Took a great big dive
And oh man alive
The golden handshake
Turned out to be a fake.

Euro was a bad word;
Sure, it turned out to be no good,
Back in came immigration.
Beg, steal again, a temptation.

Put your trust only in God.
That's my word.
The streets are not paved with gold.
The Sovereignty have debts untold.
The Celtic Tiger came and went
But Jesus, God's Son, was sent.
Yes, I know He also went

but The Good News is
He is coming back soon.

If you put your trust in
Anything else
It will be your ruin.

My maternal grandparents
Charles and Ellen North

Childhood

That old house
That hides the secrets from the past,
That linger there to last:
In every room
Hangs the gloom
That has its victims in doom.

There I would not like
To sleep in a room.
Outside, the Crossroads,
Inside, hanging all our old coats.

The long walks to school
Where by the rod they rule.
"Put out your hand, you fool,"
Said the old teacher ever so cool;
Standing in the playground,
Trouble could be found.

Too many bullies hang around:
Kneel down to take a drink
From the old bucket
That was twisted and crooked.

All I wanted was a cup
To get a drop;
There was no toilet outside
As behind the bushes we did hide.

The books were dirty and old,
The school room bare and cold;
There was a dunce's corner,
To this I was no foreigner.

Home through the old town,
Mother warned, "Don't hang around,
Pick up some bread,
Come home and be fed."

Our livelihood had to be won:
"Get sticks from the wood.
They're no good, they won't burn.
Drag water from the well."
I was nervous in case in I fell.
"Go to visit Auntie Nell,
Beg, steal and borrow,
Otherwise there will be no tomorrow."

Back to school
To be treated like a fool;
The long weary journey
Often cold and hungry.

Despite all this
We put up the fist
And to God be the glory
That I am alive
To tell the story.

Cold was the weather
But we were all together;
All we had was a candle light
As mother told stories
By the fire at night,
We drank our tea
From jam jars.
We had no cups, you see.

As the candle light faded
Off to bed we all waded.
Another day we lived.
To God the glory we give.

Tom

The spring in his step has long gone;
Of him she was very fond,
With his green twinkling eyes
He was not beyond telling lies
To cover up his shame.
Not an easy man to tame,
He made everyone feel ill at ease
Before he took then on, to tease.
This gave him a lot of control;
Their emotions are turmoiled
He was a hard man to work out;
Through town and country he got about,
Leaving behind a trail of deceit,
Many a person he did defeat.

They say it's a long road without a turn:
You'd think a man in his heart would yearn
To return to his homeland,
His family to defend.
It was not the case
With this man with
The twinkling green eyes
Who built castles in the skies.
No matter how hard you tried
You couldn't get through to him
If you cried.
He was on his own trip,
Drinking made him tired to kip
Under the starlight
Till God's day bright.
Unshaven, what a sight,
Bitter, turned his night.
Seeing him, what a fright.

Old Mrs Fagin

Old Mrs Fagin
She was a pagan;
She brought up her Son,
Now he is gone
Far across the stream
To find his dream.
She could have found God:
That's what it's all about.
She hung on to what
She was handed down;
She was lost, not found.
She could have taught
Her Son,
But now he is gone.

Old Mrs Fagin was
A pagan, always raging,
Couldn't make much sense
The other side of the fence.
The missions came and went,
Now she is old and bent.
Across the stream her son was seen
Drinking and sinking,
He never found his dream:
On the wrong side it would seem.
His Mother; she failed,
Gone off the rail;
Not much hope, for his
Light is dim.

From him, she hid the truth,
Gave him the booth;
Now she is old and frail,
Her son, gone off the rail.

He will never come home;
Now she is old, she is all alone.
The message was preached,
But she never reached out to God
Her Heavenly Lord.
She preferred her own superstitions,
That's what put her in this position;
Won't admit she is wrong
For so long.

Turn and follow Jesus, and be found.
He died on the Cross for all her loss,
He can redeem her every dream,
Put her wise to the enemy's schemes
If she could pray for her Son,
Because GOD'S SON has won.

Mr White

I followed White through the darkest night,
He was out of sight;
This man ran so fast
He was always first, never last.

He ran away from what I hold dear;
Was he cunning or was it fear?
That took him far and never near.

He ran with the wild pack
And never looked back,
His father's name was Jack.
Over the years my brain I did rack:
What was this man's lack?
He sure had a lot of slack.

He was a man on the run,
Looking for a lot of fun,
He liked a lot of drink;
He wasn't a Man to think,
Or he might have returned home.

Not left them all alone
As he went out to roam.
Paddy, Daddy, send some money tome
And leave the drinking boys alone,
As you go from bar to bar
You have taken things too far;
You are sinning through the night.

Boy, you haven't got a light,
You are in the wrong fight;
St Patrick's day with a weed in your coat,

You are not long off the Irish boat.
You are not a single man,
Leave the women alone if you can.

You were brought up in a Catholic land,
Now you are giving the single boys a hand.
You call it the craic*;
Boy, it shows your lack:
What about the wife way back?

You think you are right, Mr White,
You are walking in the dark;
Every morning you're up with the lark
And go to work in the dark.
There you carry your heavy load
Digging up the English road.

You lived with a woman who wasn't your wife;
This brought you all your strife.
You couldn't hide your pride,
Although you were walking on the wrong side
Listening to all the Irish bands;

You were one of their greatest fans,
Spending all your money on beer.
Your wife and family lived over yonder in fear;
You were a married man,
Now you have to carry the can.

You were full of folly:
What a wally.
God will relent,
After all, He shines his light on Mr White;

---

* Craic is a term for news, gossip, fun and entertainment, particularly in Ireland

He knows you lost your way,
You have always been lost:
Jesus paid the cost
On the cross.

You were not known for being wise;
You were a married man in disguise,
Chasing the women and the highs.

After all, you built a wall,
Hoping it would cover your fall:
Now you can hear God call.
He will catch you when you fall,

His love is yours and all;
But obey His call,
He knows your every sin,
He will judge you in the end.

Jesus is the Light
That will guide you through the darkest night;
Mr White, your life was a sight,
But God put you right.

The Irish Hills

The Irish hills are green,
The best ever seen;
The Liffey flowing and the stream,
Although emigration took me away
In foreign lands to stray.

I wander back in my sleep
On those green hills to creep,
And once again to peep
At the old Irish cottage below.

Then my heart begins to flow
And the vision of mother
And the young ones below,
Playing among the meadow
At our house in Caddagh.

O dear God, I pray,
Please let me stay
With the ones I love so well
Before emigration fell
And the old mail boat was there as well.

A carpet of snow fell to the ground,
And with hardly a pound,
We set sail.
The Irish sea was rough that night
As we took our flight:
All we left behind
Were our footprints in the snow.
I will remember that, wherever I go,
And in a foreign land
We put our stake.

Gone was the land of the shamrock and the snake
And the things that live deep in its wake.
But in my dreams
Run over the streams,
And once again I am a child
Under God's beams,
Only to wander back in my sleep, dreams
And try to keep under God's beams,
Those childhood memories to keep it seems.

These are the closest things to my heart
That welcomely invade my sleep.
I thank God that You will keep
Those dear ones in my sleep, sleep,
They're yours to keep.

The Wimpey Boy

Wimpey always gave the sub:
It was only a few bob
For working on the job
After leaving Ireland's bog

Wimpey imports more Paddies every year
Keeping them on the beer;
Stop him going further,
Keep him working harder.

A lack of education
Kept Paddies rolling into the stations
Of the mail boat
Like a wild goat.

Sure there's plenty more
Where he came from:
Paddy, Mick or Tom.
There's no work where
They come from.

Send a few bob home;
Through England they roam.
The beer and the craic
Stopped you going back
As you listened to the Irish songs.

For your homeland
Your heart did long.
But it was only a passing thing,
You treated life like a fling.

The roses grew up on
The house so tall,
Reaching down the wall.
The memories grew dim.
The past you put out on a limb.

Now there's no going home,
Although you are very much alone:
The passing years and the unshed tears
For the cottage on the hill.
There time stood still,
The old folks long gone,
So now you have to go on.

Now the Wimpey boys are lying low,
Some to an early grave did go,
The craic and the beer took its toll;
Maybe it would be better
Back home on the dole.

Now Paddy has to slow down;
His fading years under the British Crown.
He survived the Wimpey boys;
By their memories
He sometimes cries.

He worked hard,
Drank hard,
Played every card;
Now he stands alone,
The lining of his pockets torn.
He is in an old folks home,
His wife and kids not known.

He needs help wherever he goes.
This is heartbreak hotel,
Last stop before hell:
He cannot now turn to God –
In life he fell.

But there is hope:
A few years ago he came forth,
Accepted Jesus as his only hope;
Now Jesus will stand as his Friend
When he reaches the end:
As his Saviour will defend
The Wimpey boy in the end.

In Old Delvin

There was little food,
The kids were rude,
"You have no dad,"
Said the young lad.
"What do you know?
Just watch how you go,"
I said as I kept
Up my head.
"Sure we all have a Dad."

No, don't be misled,
The kids gathered around
The dirty old town.
No one had a bob;
Too young to take a job.
Some gathered in the street,
Hardly a shoe on their feet.
Some took a puff from a Woodbine,
The kids watched from behind.

"Here's Master Molloy.
"Come on, lads, let's fly."
Miss Cox said,
"Beg your pardon,"
Who threw the fag in her rose garden?

Simon at Delvin Church 2006

A Begging Letter from an Irish Mother to Her Son Who is Drinking Too Much, "Come on Back, God Loves You, So Do I."

Caid mela failta row,[*]
The craic is over now.
He hung out in the pub,
The boys lived above,

---

[*] Gaelic for *A hundred thousand welcomes*

He thought he was in clover,
Handing it all over.
The landlord got rich;
The craic is over now.

Paddy let his hair down
Living under the British crown;
His hard labour in vain,
His years now in twain,
And the craic is over now.

Paddy's been a fool
Sitting on that high stool,
Putting down all that Guinness;
Surely hell is in it.

Caid Mela Failta row:
Depart from that show,
The craic is over now
And time is running low.

You don't know friend or foe,
All those years sitting high;
Time has gone by
And the craic is over now.

There never was a craic: looking back
You laboured in vain,
Going through all that pain.
The landlord got rich,
You got off the pitch.

All that Guinness got you,
And you're not the man I knew.

The craic is over now;
Hand it over now,
All that money you blow.

Time is running out;
Hand it over now.

You were merry,
You were mad
And badly misled.
How can you forget
The mother who beget?

Come on, Paddy, the craic is over now;
Hand it over now,
You are not in clover now,
Hand it over now.

Don't turn your back,
God has a life for you
That is fair and true:
The craic is over now.

God knows how, and it's all over now;
Sons, come on back,
Give up the Irish craic
And tricksey at the back.

Time is knocking on the door,
God loves you more;
Life for you begins now,
So hand it over now:
The craic is over now.

REPENT

Ireland

Land of potatoes, you will learn
And not be deceived,
Sold out to wrong beliefs.
Be transformed and renewed
By the truth.
Jesus said "I am the way, the truth and the life."
God has a plan for the Irish,
To save them
From lies, deception and unbelief.

God's people are in prison
And have gone astray for lack
Of knowledge.
St Patrick?
The Irish have been deceived;
Misled, made to look foolish
All over the world.

It's now time to waken up
And face the truth.
God never intended the Irish people
To get drunk and disorderly, all
In the name of one of His saints.
St Patrick was sent to Ireland
To bring the people to God,
To teach them the Gospel of Jesus
And lead them to God.

A gospel of love, joy, peace;
A far cry from being drunk and disorderly.
Ireland may very well be having
A great time now
Living in the wealth of the great economy
Of this day,

But it has a lost generation of young people
Who have lost their way.
The rich economy has the people blind to
The real agony of the young who are walking
In the dark.
The Catholic Church does not have the answer
To the problems of the day,

Only God can help the Irish
Come out of the terrible deception
Of the St Patrick celebrations
And the wrong being committed
By such a wrong celebration.
This is only the tip of the deception
That the Irish are living in;

God calls His people to come out
And touch no unclean thing,
And He will receive you.
Be set free and, by His truth,
Salvation is the only answer.

Bernie (left) and Terrence White

Ballin Valley

I went to Ballin Valley school.
They thought I was a fool.
They closed the door and
Locked me away all day.
I don't feel sorry for myself;
My education was put on the shelf.

The poor kids came from the Spike;
It was them I came to like.
We all played together,
In cold and windy weather.
We walked a long way home.
Threw the odd stone.

Lonely walks
With no talks
Through the country roads.
We carried our painful loads
Of sorrow that was deep and true.
Sometimes we walked with
The kids we knew.

They often called me names
Or played silly games.
I wanted to get on,
Sing the odd song,
After them trail along.
They often didn't want this.
They got angry, put up the fist.

I never failed to see
How odd they could be.
What was their problem anyway?

We all walked there every day.
The same old shoes,
the same old blues.
We couldn't choose.

If you don't go to school
The Guards will lock you away.
Mother shouted after us every day.
Don't mitch, or hide in the ditch.

The teacher who taught us
Fought us.
Sometimes she beat us with a stick.
The big kids also gave us a kick.

The village had its monthly Fair,
Selling cows from Kildare.
Walk through them if you dare.
The smell of stale beer
Had me locked in fear
As the farmers clapped
Each others' hand
When a sale did land.

The higgler sold his eggs
From a table with only three legs.
The bob man sold the odd milk can.
The Fair over, the farmer half- sober.
He called his dog Rover.

The streets left full of cows' poo.
Come on lad, clear it up,
You have nothing else to do.

On his foot he hadn't got a shoe.
The farmer threw him a bob or two.
Delvin 1958.
What a state.

Poverty Lurks

Me, with my father (early '90s)

In dusty hills
I walk alone,
Because I didn't
Come home.
In such bad times
There wasn't a dime
To spend on life
For child or wife.

To beg for bread
So the hungry could be fed
Was a daily task.
It hurt, to ask.
Many knew,
To our door, came few
Offering a helping hand.

After all this was hospitable Ireland
To God be the glory.
He let me live
To tell this story.

I crawled on my hands and knees
Begging God 'please:
Have mercy on us
For it's with a great thirst,
I come to You first.
Help us all to survive,
Not run away and hide'.

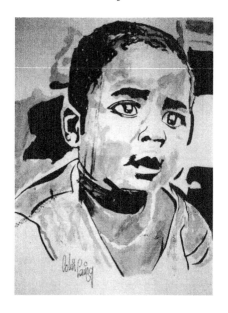

Father went away,
Hasn't returned to this day.
He got led astray,
For sin with him had its way.
For this he must pay.

His conscience came late.
He forgot his faith.
Even God had to wait
For this sinner to return
Or in hell's fire burn.
In the end he gave in,
Packed up all his sin.
God will always win;
He died for his sin.

Don't Waste Another Day

Don't waste another day,
Come and walk this way;
I called you by your name,
Tomorrow I will say it again.
You are my greatest friend,
The path has been set near;
I know I made it clear:
I will not lose,
You are the very one I choose.

Look over your shoulder,
You are my soldier;
I have dressed you for the part,
Given you a brand new heart,
No more looking back,
I've wiped your past away:
Now come and walk this way.
You have all you need,
And from My Word you are to feed
Those walking in great need.

Teach my people to read,
Not just to listen
but to heed
And when the battle passes over
Those you draw to me I cover;
I take them by the hand
To an Eternal land,
And there they live forever
Under My righteous hand.

Once a Lowly Beggar

Once a lowly beggar
And now a traveller for God;
I waited for many a year
And then I saw a tear
Fall from the sky
And on the ground it lay to cry.

It came down from heaven
And just dropped by,
And then another fell too
Just to remind me and you:
It was a tear or two, so true
Of a pain that caused great gain.

No, it was not a drop of rain,
I know this to be so because I
Was lying low,
With nowhere in this world to go,
Kneeling on my bended knees
Begging God "Please,
I know You're there, but show
Me that You care,
For You know that I am Your
Lowly servant begging here."

It's a long time since I've eaten
And I feel poorly and beaten;
The world is a big, big place
And there's so much space,
Now I am on bended knees
Longing to be free.
Show me the way to be free,
Show me the way to go
So that I won't have to lie low;

Send me some bread so that I am fed.
I already know Your word
And won't let go;
I surrender all that I am to Your
Loving care,
Because I know that You're there.
Down here in this world I am treated
So unfair
By those who are unloving and dare.
But You, O my God, up there
With Your tender loving care
Won't let me be unjustly lost.

You have already died for me on the cross
And You feed me and weed me
So that I am clean and bright,
And now You feed me and I am no longer a sight.
If any more people reach this point
And realise they are dirty and hungry and unkempt,
God has looked after me all these years;
His intention was always, you see
To set me totally free:
But first I felt the pain of being lost.
Now I no longer waste time
walking down that dirty line.

God, show me a new way to go
Where *heavenly waters* flow
So that I am no longer lying low.
I am teaching His Word wherever I go;
That is what He told us to do, you know:
He said: "Go ye therefore and teach all nations."
And I take Him at His word
And love everyone. A command:

Walk in faith. It pleases God.
See I am a woman under authority – God's.
I walk in obedience.

In the '80s

Broken Kid

In times gone by
I sat and cried
For my Daddy far away,
Wondering why
He didn't stop by.
The weeks, months, years
All flew by,
He didn't drop in to say Hi
To the girl or boy,
As time went on.
My childhood all gone,
I was working for a song
When he dropped along.
Gone was the hope of long ago
As I sat in the old bus station,
My heart a-racing.
In the crowd I saw his face:
Gone was the dark hair;
You couldn't tell if
He was dark or fair.
He put on a lot of weight
As he walked through the gate
With a faded smile.
I looked away for a while
As this, the daddy, I waited
So long to see.
He is older,
That's the key;
His youth in decay,
My childhood passed away.
It was a greeting
Long waited for.
In his eyes, sorrow.
"Daddy you are lost."

Drink, what a cost.
Bloodshot eyes
Leave no disguise.
Your mother died
when you were four,
Leaving you troubles galore.
You carried the pain,
To get rid of it was in vain;
The love of a wife and kids
Couldn't get rid.
In you was the broken kid;
Now I have to forgive,
Let live.
For my childhood was stolen
As home drunk you came rolling.
You were more inclined
To go the way
That was wrong
Without a mother's guiding hand
For so long.

When God gives love
Straight from above
To help me through,
I tried to pass it on to you.
You were a broken man,
As all the world could see.
How could you be a daddy to me?
Now that you are gone,
Time to think so long,
I saw you shed your tears,
Talk about all your fears,
Missing out on all our years.
We all meet half way
That day,

In a Dublin Tea house.
We sat down
With mixed emotions
And a frown;
You worked under the British Crown,
You were still short of the pound.
The mail-boat in sight,
Now over was half the fight:
Still to come was the darkest night.
Another time about that
I will write.
The dawn was now in sight,
And we would all take flight
To an English shore:
We would go galore.
Then Father would take flight,
Then became our darkest night.
Two more would board:
We had a heavy load.
Bristol was our destination;
Father returned to Kent
Where his youth was spent.
Through tears and tears,
Troubles and woes,
On the White family goes.
The pirates came on board,
One by one,
Oh what a heavy load.
The battle began,
We didn't have the sense to run;
It would be a long time
Before we broke loose
From the Lacheco noose.
We got caught up,
That put a stop

To our dreams.
If a broken man's schemes,
He rolled on
With his family gone.
This was the outcome
Of the broken kid's life,
Forsaking kids and wife.
So now we roll on,
He is long gone.
Let us all forgive,
Now live.
God will give,
His love will live.
Now, if you can't forgive,
Then God can't forgive you;
So you are standing in
Your own way,
Blocking yourself in:
That's a sin.
It's human to err,
Divine to forgive;
So come on, forgive
And live.
God will give,
He is Divine and love
Entwined.
Get all wrapped up in
His Love.
There will be
No Daddy's love,
But sure, a great big
Daddy is up above,
Willing to give you His love.
God is His Name.
He loves us all the same.

GANGSTER

Wild Goose

The Wild Goose is
An old pub house
Where we may wander
In, sit and ponder,
And after we go there
Some kneel and say a prayer.

A place to meet;
A place to greet,
A place to rest our weary feet.

Often we have been forgotten,
Downtrodden.
So give a thought
For what ought
When the wild goose got caught,
To rest their weary head,
And off the street get led.

God help them all get fed.
To trust more in God as He loves them,
Where strangers may meet
And friends re-treat,
On Stapleton Road, street,
The Wild Goose
In the old public house.

As I walk in
There is a lot of talk.
The food laid on the plate.
We all queue up,
No time to wait.

We took our seat,
There to retreat
And food to eat.
We carry our sorrow
Right into tomorrow.

Don't you know
We have no home anyway,
For things slipped away
One day,
Like water through my
Fingers.
I tried to hold on
But it was gone.

So be alert:
The meek shall inherit
The earth.

The Black Flash

It was a midnight treat
When I landed on my feet
On skid-row street.
I bought the booze,
Win or lose,
I didn't have a buck:
Everyone took a good look.

My light was dim
When I bumped into him;
He was the black flash
Used to dealing with others' trash.
He could pull a knife,
Take another man's life
If a man only blinked an eye:

See his life passing by.
This man stood tall
Against the dark wall;
He dressed very well,
Beside him many men fell.
He charged a fee,
Said "Man, come follow me
For I haven't ever lost a fight.
I got to watch my back,
Get up with the lark,
Hide in the dark.
I have a fierce punch,
See a man's bones crunch.
I do not flight,
But always fight.
If you hang out with me
You will never be free,
For a rebel's reward you will get,
Always full of fret,
Lots of regret.
I have a dark past,
Out of society I have been cast;
All my own doing,
It will be the day of my ruin.
Drink up your booze,
Win or lose,
Be always confused,
I answer to no man.
All of them I out-ran.
Now you are bust.
In the morning you will still have your thirst.
Skid row on will flow.
You will be hated
Wherever you go.
Your past

Will outlast.
You are a thief,
You will never sleep,
Giving people all that grief.

Listen to what the preacher man said
And don't be misled.
Clean up your act:
I am lost, that's a fact.
You know Jesus saved the thief on the cross.
You can turn over a new leaf
If you go follow Him,
Your light won't be dim.
Hey, don't worry about me,
I know Jesus can set me free.
This is my last night on skid row:
Now watch how you go,
No need to hang low,
I am giving up the way I go.
Turning around was slow.

I am no longer the *Black Flash*.
A while ago a man did slash
My right arm; took all my cash,
Forty stitches later I lost the flash,
I found my Waterloo.
Now all I can do
Is stand and talk to you
And what I tell you is true.

What Jesus done for me, He will do for you:
He lit up my path,
Took all my wrath
That was due to me.
He let me go free.

I have turned around,
Took another route,
Gave the enemy the boot,
Now I am growing like a new shoot,
Gone is the inner brute.

Now I spread the word
About the saving Lord
Who will come to save the world.
At our darkest hour,
Down his love will shower.
He sent to flight
My darkest night,
Turned me from wrong to right.
He pulled me in; put up a fight
To save my soul that night
When a man more fierce than me
To end my life, he held the key.
But I lived to tell the tale
Of what will happen when a man goes off the rail.

Now I preach Jesus on skid row
Or wherever else I go.
No more Black Flash
Carrying all that trash:
My Lord and Saviour Jesus
Is what pleases
My heart, my soul, my all.

The Prisoner

I sat on a lonely prison chair;
It was then I realised there was no one there.
As the big doors closed loud in my ears
It seemed to release all my hidden fears.
I heard the footsteps of the prison screw walking away:
He had other inmates to treat this way.
I heard more big doors slam that night;
Sure I know I am in here because I didn't do right.

It was lonely that night when the light went out,
I lay there on my pillow; all I could do was shout;
The hidden heartaches all seemed to come out.
They taunted me throughout the night:
All the time I did wrong when I could have done right.
The memories that bloated my mind,
Heartaches of a different kind.

Too often we keep the box and throw away the gift;
Now I am searching my mind to see, what I can shift
And make it like a well ordered room:
If I can throw out all the dark and gloom.

I meet an inmate: he said he is going out soon.
Back to your old ways, I did groom.
He threw a long look across the room.
"Take a good look at my face," he said.
There were big tears dropping down
"Oh no, my friend, I am no clown,"
He said, looking down to the dirty ground.
"I have spent ten stolen years in this prison place,
Got my head messed up out of space.
I had a good family,
They thought the world of me.

I was so young and so free;
I spent all my liberty
Drifting through the streets,
Picking up all the treats.
Little did I know that is where I would find all my defeats.

"No, man, I ain't going back to the streets,
Don't want to pick up no dirty treats.
I am going to find me a great big church;
There, I am going to pray for these I left in the lurch.
My family have all moved on,
Couldn't take their son being a con.

"I need God to forgive all my sins;
Clean me without and within;
Set me free
From the heart-aches that trouble me.

"No man, I ain't no clown no more,
Not like I used to be before.
You see, my friend, I found Jesus;
He accepted me.
You see, that's why I am free
While still inside prison."

Now I return to my own cell,
Thinking about this fellow, he sure rang a bell,
And, by all accounts, he has sure ran from hell.

What God has done for this here man
I know He can do for me.

Tiny Feet

Tiny feet that once walked this street:
Who took God out of the school,
Turned your son into a fool?
He wears a hood, thinks life is no good,
He takes a gun, shoots your son, thinks it's fun.
Come on, think before we sink. It's late in the day.

Think.
Was he a latch door kid?
By whom was he fed?
Come on, think. Make that vital link.

He hides under that hood.
It's no good, he smokes that yoke,
Gung on his throat
Come on think, make that link.
Running feet that darken our street,
The hooded boy with the darken eye
The hardened heart standing in the dark,
The faded hood:
This is no good.
Come on, think, the dope got that bloke,
His mind desensitised. Will he rise out of the gutter?
There is no disguise. It's got the guys. Come on, *think*.
The boy on the bike, he's got the gear,
Rob, rob, rob, it's dear.

Maybe your hair won't be grey.
You'll die on the way;
You meddled with the devil's tool,
Became a walking fool.
Wake up before it's too late.
Come on, be good and wait.
Suffer the symptoms to withdraw
Come on, before you fall.

Jesus has a love for you,
A love that's so true;
Why give it all away
And not live to see another day?
What is it that's hurting you?
Come, talk, do it for you;

Don't lock it up, throw away the key.
Come on now and do the deal,
Get it off your chest,
You'll see that's for the best.
What do you carry in your heart
That's pulling you apart?
Come, lay it all down,
Don't let it put you in the ground.

A promise for you,
Only if you do
Talk it all away.
Don't carry this day.
Jesus has a love for you
A love that is so true.
Come lay it all down
Then you turn around.
You will have a clean slate,
Not tripping on the devil's bait.
You never knew a better way,
Come on, live today
The road you walk is full of evil talk,
Come with Jesus, now walk, talk.
You've been going astray,
Come now, live today.
I know that inside you're good,
Give up the bad you should;
Maybe you're hurting inside.
Come on, don't run and hide,
Come talk it all away
Then all will be ok.

Wouldn't Walk the Line

Hey, man, wouldn't walk the line,
Lazing around, getting up at nine;
Thought I knew best
Hanging out with the rest.
Thought my homey had a plan,
Then I fell again;
I ran with the gang.

Bang, bang, bang,
My homey hit the ground;
Oh man, what a pound.
The ringing of the bang
Out where we hang;
The smell of the dirty street
Where once ran tiny feet.

I am full of fear
Running for my gear;
Met the guy
With the devil in his eye.
He stuck out his hand,
I though he had a plan.
All he wanted was my money,
Then he went a-running.
I kicked up a fight,
Couldn't see no light;
My mind was full of haze
Walking in a daze.
Pulled on my hood:
God, help me if You would.

I am staring into space
Lost the living place.
Now I am on the street
With the whole fleet.
I really did it this time.
Wouldn't walk the line.
Under my coat got a gun.
Now I am on the run.
Got to let the gear go,
Got to say no,
Got to mean it in my heart.

And I got no life
Carrying this knife.
It's all down to the gear
And the dreadful fear;
If I meet the gang on the other patch
Will he pull the latch,
Leave me on the street
Where once ran tiny feet?
Got to say No,
Go and hang low,
Give it all up, let it go:
Rise to the top,
Yeah, got to stop.

The Hooded Guy with the Darkened Eye

The hooded guy with the darkened eye,
He has been living a lie;
He stalks the streets
With tired feet,
He got to get the gear,
Running in great fear.
With friend or foe
His options are running low,
His anger getting high,
The limit is the sky.
Got to get the message through:
I need the gear, I do.

The streets of St Paul's
That's where I get it all;
I have been tripping on the devil's bait,

Maybe I left it too late.
Death knocking on the door,
O My God, what have You in store?
I have been living a lie
Though I could reach the sky.
Got in with the bad boy,
Now I need to run and hide;
All last night I cried,
Never thought I could reach this place,
My head is out of space,
Kicked my granny in the face
Trying to get money in her place.
She never stopped loving me;
She is aware I am not free,
Caught up in this blasted crack:
How I wish I could give it back.

The rest of the family
Have turned their back on me.
Maybe it can't get any worse than this,
My granny didn't deserve to get the fist:
She was there for me in my childhood,
Always said I was good.
What have I done?
Thought it was fun,
Now I am on the run
Carrying a loaded gun;
Family think I am a bum.
"Mother dear, I am your son
Didn't mean to hit your mum.
I carried her in my heart,
Never knew that we would part.
Now it's too late,
She has passed the eternal gate."

With tears in my eyes
I am falling from the sky;
I hit rock bottom,
Not a penny in my pocket.
"Please, My Jesus, forgive me
And set me free.
You know I am lowly in my heart:
That's what's tearing me apart."
What I said from the start,
I was the guy with the darkened eye;
My dreams falling from the sky,
Living the dreary lie,
Lashing out at my granny in the eye.

Now the game's all up:
I took time to get right with God.
You know the writing was on the wall,
Gave up the gear,
Stopped running in fear.
Jesus has made me clean,
Now to live, I am keen.
Sorry, Mummy dear,
Now you don't need to live in fear,
Your son's off the gear.
I am now the hooded guy,
Jesus' love looking through my eye.

The Dope's Got the Bloke

The dope got the bloke,
The bloke got the dope;
They sell it to the fool,
It's the devil's tool.
You will lose your mind,
This you will truly find
Your mind cannot take.
Give it up for God's sake,
You will get mentally ill,
The Barrow wards you will fill,
Your family's heart will break:
Give it up for God's sake.

The years will pass away,
Your hair turning silver grey,
It will bring a hopeless day.
Don't give it all away,
You only got one life,
Why put in the knife,
Why sell your soul,
And not reach your life goal?.

God paved your way,
Come on, live another day;
The poison filters through,
Who is to blame, but you?
In streets where once stood tiny feet
No time to talk the fleet.
Someone is dead. That's too bad;
Got to do the deal,
Don't care what you feel,
High as a kite,
Streets full of fight.

Come on, think,-
Make that vital link:
The growers the goers.
It will bring you low,
Come on, think,
It's on the door;
There's a price to pay
For lapsing this day:
Up at the top the cats are fat,
Down below they're dying galore.

The Petition

Went down to Easton,
There I went feasting:
St Werburgh's is down the road.
From St Paul's I carried my load,
I know my way around,
I walk a lot of ground,
Don't waste no time
Looking for my homey, to find
The cops on every corner,

My homey sends out a warning:
"Take the lane through Ashley Down,
Other ways, man, you will be found.
You get us into trouble,
Hey, man, don't burst my bubble.
You cut through Gloucester Road,
Man don't lose the load.
You know I got to pay my way,
Oh, man, gets me through the day,
I got men waiting for the gear.
Come on, mate, don't fill me with fear,
Time is money, man, that ain't funny:
You know I got a flash car."

My homey thinks that is going too far.
I don't live in Easton,
I only go there to feasting,
Coupled with the fact I am a pimp;
One of catches got a limp.
One of the guys flying in
With a pony in his bin;
It's worth a lot o dough,
Man, that is why I am hanging low.
Last week three guys died,
Now I have to hide;
The gear was too cool,
The fat cat was a fool
Giving us faulty tool.

Man, the guilt is heaping up,
Some time I think I got to stop;
Got too many guys on the payroll
As well as picking up the dole;
Got money coming out my ears,
But hey, man, I am full of fears,

Ain't no joke tripping on the devil's gear.
My house is full of tears,
My woman's ready to walk out on me,
Says she wants to set me free,
Says I am a hound dog,
And in my mouth I got a log.
If I could analyse her talk,
Hey, man, maybe it's better to walk;
Can't expect her to wait
To see the outcome of my fate;
Now I wish I had faith.
Ah, man, do you think it's too late?
I look up to the sky,
I am a lowly, lowly guy.

O my God, I don't want to die,
Firing bullets while I am high.
I am running through the lanes,
Carrying all my pains;
The gear is tearing me apart,
Pulling on strings of my heart.
Went a-feasting in Easton,
Running through the lanes,
Carrying al my pains,
As well as a gun,
Always on the run.
I am an inner city bum,

Came from Trinidad, when I was only a lad;
They taught me to be a good boy;
But look at me, on drugs I got high.
I don't want my boy to be like me,
Want him to be free;
Don't want him running through the lanes
Carrying no pains,

Don't want him to go by the graveside
Telling his buddies how his dad got high.

Now he dies
And turns others' life upside down,
Found lying in the gutter ground.
That ain't loving, my son,
Carrying the loaded gun;
Where did it all go wrong?
It's been like that too long.

Had a happy childhood,
Mummy taught me to be good,
She took me to church,
Never left me in the lurch;
I got bullied at school,
Made to feel a fool,
No one took my part.
Maybe this was the start,
Fell down in my heart,
I lost my hope,
My senses seemed to elope.
I am not the man my daddy brought me up to be,
He must feel let down by me;
He doesn't talk to me anymore,
When we meet he looks down to the floor.
I think I made him lose his hope,
My poor daddy, he is a sad bloke.
And my mother's eyes are full of sorrow,
I wish I could promise her a better tomorrow;
I am breaking their hearts,
That is now tearing them apart.
I have lied,
Ran and hide,
Love will never die.

Now I am on my knees,
Begging God, "Please,
Don't turn Your back on me.
Please set me free
For my lowly days,
All my wicked ways."
Then Jesus whispered in my heart,
"Come on, My son, of My kingdom be part.
Of course I forgive you from the start,
Now we will never part,
I will give you a brand new start and heart;
Of My kingdom be part.

Go now, you have My love.
Be gentle as a dove,
Meek as a child;
Spread My word and My love,
I'll be watching you from above.
I will guide you through,
You will not stumble or fall;
My son, you heard My call.
You have the great commission;
Now for human souls go fishing."

Jesus heard your petition.

The Cop's Got the Gun

The kids running wild;
Can't be satisfied.
The cop's got a gun,
He will shoot your son,
Running through the street
There will be no defeat.

It's a battle no one can win,
The dope's in the big wheelie bin.
Search, search don't give up,
The neighbours have had enough,
There are lanes running through.
Come on, run from the boys in blue.

No, no stop, I just
Heard a shout.

It's our buddy. He's dead.
Oh I wish by God
We were led;
The street, it's paved with red.
The boy is left for dead.

I know I should have kept the law,.
Now I am feeling raw;
Sitting in the cell
I can hear the bell.

People outside going to church,
But I am locked here in the lurch.

I got time to think:
Oh boy, the toilet, what a stink.

I got a single chair;
Out there, does anyone care?

My buddy's on my mind,
We didn't walk the line.
My buddy was black
And I am white,
On the streets we
Took our fight.
Now he's out of sight.
Wish we didn't fight.

We grew up in Easton,
On its prey we went a-feasting.
Meet the boys from St Paul's,
Stuck around, that's all;
After a while into
Drugs we begin to dive.

Into St Werburgh's we
Took the alley and the lane;
Now it's full of pain.

Didn't know the cop had a gun
When we went on the run;
We were full of fun
As we dished out the gear.
Life was passing us by.

You see, I am white
And put up a fight.

I am the apple of God's eye,
He is looking down from the sky;
He loves me now,

As well as bye and bye.
O God, take away
The fear: my buddy
Dead, the price is high.

The Bounty Hunter

Who is the bounty hunter
That follows me country to country?
Got off with me at every station,
Stayed with all my relations.
Was it by the price on my head
That he was greedily led?

If I didn't commit the crime,
Out of me he wouldn't make a dime;
But I have done the deed
That will finally meet his need.

I have to say it's all my trash
That will finally make him some cash;
But first I have to be his catch.
So I was on the ball
When I received his call.

"Hey, man, where you hangin' out?"
"None your business," down the line I shout.
That was a close one.
Outside the sun shone,
No time to take a kip,
I need to make a trip.

My funds are running low
Plus I have nowhere to go.
I fear, not to be led back
He will be on my track;
I got to keep running,
That guy is very cunning.

My life of crime
I would like to leave behind;
But I will never be free
While he is hunting me.

It's time to give myself up,
Stop living wild and rough.
I kneel to say a prayer:
"Dear God, up there,
They tell me that You care.

I have been a fool.
Thought I was cool,
I promise to stop:
Give it all up,
Turn my life around."

Now that I know Jesus
I am found;
Now I will hand myself in,
Get in touch with my kin,
For it was all my sin.

But in the end
Jesus my soul did win,
For the bounty hunter's loss
Has at last come to the cross.

Wacky Backy

Give up the wacky backy,
Your lungs do not appreciate
Being in this state:
They are struggling in your chest,

Trying to find rest,
You put them to the test;
Now they are in a mess:
Can't you see the light?

Your lungs, dark as the night,
Never meant to get them in this state:
Just pray it's not too late.
After all they are only flesh.

Come on, give it up, that's best;
What a task,

Your face cooled in a mask,
Having your mind altered.

Falling by the way, you faltered,
Wouldn't take no heed;
Come on, give up the weed,
It will be for the best.

Give your chest a rest,
Keep on plugging through,
You know what it will do:
You will die, mate.

Living on a cold slate,
You were put to the test,
You wouldn't listen.
Now go and rest forever, in your tomb.

A fool since you left the womb,
God has a better plan;
Come on, live it, you can,
Don't be a rebel,

Relying on a pebble,
Come on, you let a weed
Turn your life into a seed.
Give it up, come on, stop.

The weed will fill your brain,
It will not take away the pain;
In your life, there will be no gain:
Come on, deal with the pain.

What was it that cut you through and through?
Something you didn't do?

Don't let the devil trick you;
Yes, that's what he plans to do.

The weed is his bait,
Don't leave it too late,
He is waiting at hell's gate:
Your soul he wants to burn.

Come on now, turn
and leave, leave, leave;
You may think it's a rave,
This weed has made you a slave.

Come on, give it up,
Think about your lungs and stop;
God will help you all the way,
I promise you that today.

Don't give it all away.
Come, live on another way;
Find God's way,
He will lead you today.

Bring Back the Kids

The lost child runs wild,
No path to follow;
Life is hollow,
They want to be free
But cannot see.
Drugs and alcohol
Is a slippery road
That leads to overload
One's life with other vices
That take away life's choices.

They run to find fun,
Only to be caught in a net
Out of which they can't get.
When will they listen?
Who will blow the whistle
Before it is too late?
Come on, don't wait,
Slow down, get out of town,
Get back in the slow lane.

I am not saying bring back the cane,
But some discipline;
All the boundaries have been taken down,
Inside, no kids have been found.
They don't go to church.
Who left them in the lurch?
Broken down homes,
The dirty streets to roam;
Mummy isn't home.
You're out all alone.

I see trouble in store
Coming home to the door;

Where are the fathers?
Lawlessness has taken over,
Everyone has run for cover,
The houses burn down,
It's not safe to go to town.
The days of riots are here;
All now live in fear.

It could break out any day;
The young have gone astray
For lack of God's knowledge
And gone the way of folly.
They have no interest,
No investment in their society.
Gone is their loyalty.

Save the kids now:
Bring back God,
Bring back love,
Bring back boundaries,
Bring back discipline,
Bring back Mummy and Daddy;
TV games, computer games have reared the kids,
They have been fed with what has misled.

Now they are robots in disguise,
Just like they are hypnotised;
They have lost all hope,
Their senses have all eloped.

Bring back the kids:
All the falsehood, get rid,
Broken down society:
Help the kids.
Tomorrow will be brighter for all

If you will take this call,
Because if the kids fall
So do we all.
Hear God's call,
He will win them all,
His love will break down the wall;
Your way will only make them fall.

Specific Topics

Mother Dear

Mother dear, why so full of fear,
Don't you know Jesus is near?
Don't close your ears,
Be so full of fears,
The love of Jesus is real.
It's all around, can't you feel?
Cast your fears on Him,
The light's not dim,

Can't you see, He sets you free?
He's holding out His hand
On Earth's land,
He is the God of the living,
Here and now, ever giving.
He loves you with an everlasting love
That comes down from above;
When hearts are broken,
He is here to heal.
His love is all around:
Can't you feel?

Cast all your cares on Him,
The light is not dim,
Trust only in Him.
He has goods in store for you
Given with a heart so true,
He has a faithful love
That comes down from above;
He is knocking on the door,

So hold out your hands
And see what lands.
All the glory to Him,
His light is not dim;
Can't you see,
He is setting you free?
Praise, glory to God:
Father, Son and Holy Spirit.

Greetings my fair ones

I met him in the grape vine,
Sipping a glass of unpolluted wine,
And I saw the sun shine over the hill behind.
I said that surely he was mine.

And our love was of a different kind.
And I wonder if he could consider me in his mind.
If we could get it right this time.
With God's love we would be bound.

In the Grape Vine him I found,
Sitting on God's holy ground,
Where the grapes flow all around.
Is his heart full of sorrow?

Surely we will have a better tomorrow.
I know that we were meant to meet.
Now the grapes they are sweet.
I take this new love to my Saviour to meet.

Knowing both of us He will greet.
After all we were destined to meet.
Let us both sit at Jesus' feet.
It's there that both of us will meet.

Walk

I've wiped your past away.
Now come and walk this way.
You have all you need,
And from My word you are to feed.

Those walking in great need
Teach My people to read,
As well as listen.
Also to heed.

When the Battle passes over,
Those you draw to Me I cover.
I'll take them by the hand,
To an Eternal Land.

There they will live forever,
Under My righteous hand.
Don't waste another day.
Come walk this way.

I called you by your name yesterday.
I said the same.
Tomorrow I will say it again.
You are my greatest friend.

The path has been set near.
I know I made it clear.
I will not lose.
You are the very one I choose.

Look over your shoulder;
You are my soldier.
I've dressed you up for the part:

Given you a brand new heart.
No more looking back.
You have got a brand new start.
Lay down your pride.
Do not hide.

You are my Bride.
Follow me, follow me.
Follow me.
Step inside. Do not hide.

I have died for you.
It is my desire
To set your heart on fire.
Let the praises flow on through.

Get rid of sin.
Put on your garments.
Serve God.
Praise God, Love God.
Wait upon the Lord.

A word from God to all.

Dreams

Your dreams and hopes unfold
In a world that's fast getting cold.
When you have shared your hurts and pain
and gone over them time and again,
You find no solution.

In this world there is so much pollution;
Everything that you held so dear
and wouldn't let go out of fear.
The Friends who listened while you bare your soul.

Let them see your turmoil unfold.
Did they pick up some pieces?
Not helping the final release,
For everyone needs to be healed.

And only the love of God can see,
Put a stop to this terrible prop
That we lean upon and are seen upon.
It's so easy not to deal.

With these things you cannot feel,
To keep them hid deep below,
And feel that nobody would ever know.
Only to God could you show.

He knows everything you know.
With Him you will grow.
He will help you through,
Make for you everything new.

Don't play games

Don't play games,
Making out I am to blame.
Don't use your wit
To drive me into a fit.
I am only a human soul.
God called me back to the fold.
Don't play games with me,
For I truly am sincere.
Don't hurt me, fill me with fear.
Remember I wear my heart on my sleeve.
Don't say you are going to leave.
Only if you mean it.
It will send me to the pit.
Once will do to say good-bye to you,
But never would be better.
Don't play games with me,

For you know that I am true,
And I am truly fond of you.
And I am truly sincere;
This I hope you will find dear.
That's why you must not play games with me.

Days gone by

On days gone by
We look back why?
Is the time being
Not worth seeing?
We either look back
Or too much ahead,
Instead.

Why can't we enjoy the now?
We need to find out how,
And learn to enjoy,
Or we will look back by and by
Only to avoid living in today.

It seems to be nature's way
Of coping with
What we cannot hold,
Which is time
That slips on by through our fingers.
No matter what we do,
It will not linger.

Then when we are old,
We will not be told
How to enfold
All that we hold:
From the past
Things that will not last.

But out we must cast,
all them fast.

How do you know?

How do you know about
My broken nights?
When all hope is out
Of sight.
When I shed my silent tears,
That I'd stored up
All these years.

When it seemed the dawn
Would never break.
I prayed, let it
For God's sake...
Don't hold back the dawn.
Let the dark night
Be gone.

I lie in this room,
With all its gloom.
Please God, I pray,
Help me soon.

Why should you know
There are men living
In death row,
For the crimes
They did commit.
Wouldn't want to be
Them, in a pit.

Without Jesus they
Went astray.
Listened to the enemy
On the way.
Then fell, destined for hell.

How long the night,
These things in sight.

The world is so astray.
Please God, help, without delay.
The long night when I
Can't put anything right.

We won't survive without
Your Light, O God.
Hear me this night
When all my fears are in sight.
Make them go in flight.

Because it's to You O God
I turn tonight.
There's nothing I can do
O God, without You.

I am in fear O God in this room,
O God will it be over soon?
Me, living in this room.

For I want to spread
My wings.
Listen how the birds
Sing.
A melody that will follow me.

Revival India

People of India
I have something to say
As I pass by this way.
Don't be misled
By the badly fed.

Turn to God
And the Living Word.
Jesus is also Your Saviour
(I am the Way, the Truth and the Life).

India's waters flow
Ever so slow,
Turning the tide of time.
Bringing changes all around.

Old things are nowhere to be found.
Broken down.
Broken down
Like an earth-quaked town,

Shattered in the past;
They couldn't last.

No more deceit,
Only growing wheat,
Parcelled up in the past.

Now new things that will last,
Handed down from God,
The Creator of all.

Raise up your head,
Eternally fed,
Plenty for all,
By the word of the living GOD.

Winter

What will this winter bring?
The birds won't sing.
Will there be snow on the ground?
Will the pond be frozen?
Will ice on the pond be found?
Will the winter seem long,
And in the birds' beak no song?

And when the spring breaks forth,
Will all the birds and animals hold court?
Will all the flowers come up
And the cold of winter stop?

Will I suffer the same old heart-ache
When I have given all, and they take?
For their own sake
Does anyone want to know how I feel

As for a moment the stage I steal
As the summer sun shines through.

I think of all the people I know;
Will they take time to make that call,
Or will silence fall
And the echoes of the past stall?

I hear the whisper as they pass bye,
And once again I can only say, why?
They all cast me aside.
Nowhere to run and hide.

The oceans deep and wide.
Sometimes out, sometimes in, the tide.
But all the time inside,
In God I will confide
All my troubles and strife.
It's only Him
When I am out on a limb.

Foster and adopt

What's up?
Too many kids in care.
It's so unfair.
There are empty homes.
People who live alone.
Take a kid out of care.
Take away the pain.
They can't bear.

It shows a lack of love
If you believe in God above.
The kids are in need
To clothe and feed,
Not to become a latch door kid.

Their parents just get rid,
So they can drink and sink.

They walk away;
Have nothing to say.
The buck stops there
And they get taken into care.
They throw away the key.
The State pays the fee.

People stray, that's the key,
From their responsibility they flee.
You have to be brave.
Only Jesus can save.

One day they may occupy
A life that's high,
Buying drugs
From the street thugs.

Who brought these kids up?
Ever told them to stop,
Their bad behaviour drop?
We have street gangs.

How the shootings range.
They shot a small kid.
We need to get rid,
Before it's too late.

They meet their fate
Outside the school gate.
They haven't grown up.
This all has to stop.

Being troubled

My troubles are here, there and everywhere.
It seems so very unfair.
What is my crime?
Do I have to do time?
Do I know who is friend or foe?
Wherever I go.

Sometimes I feel so rejected,
It seems like I have wrecked it.
Some say I should hang on.
Others say I should run along.

What's the answer to my call?
Will I run or fall?
Does anyone hear me at all,
Whenever I call?

All I want is a quiet life,
Without worry or strife.
Are my troubles in my mind?
Is that what I am searching to find?

I always look deep
When it's time to sleep.
Looking through my emotions,
Deep as the vast oceans.

There's so much I cannot say.
That's why I bottle them up this way.
If I speak in silence,
Will you hear them in the high lanes?

Will my words roam around,
Lost and never found?
If only we could speak
What's on our mind.
Would people still be kind?

I seem to sit alone in a crowd.
My silence speaks out loud.
Can you hear what I am trying to say?
My troubles at your door I will lay.

What do I have to do
To get through?
You blame it on me,
When all the time it's you?

I cannot speak my words.
I'd bottle them up if I could.
The bottle's full to the top.
Now I must give up.

Complaining I must stop;
I can't say what's on my mind.
It always comes out-
A different kind.

For Sandra in the '90s

Stars fell from the sky,
And I asked God why?
A picture that was wrong
Is now put right.

It was black,
Now it's white.
It was wrong,
now it's right.

It was full of darkness,
But now it's full of light.
It was danger,
Now God has rearranged it.

It was all upside down,
For so long going wrong.
Now it's going to be right,
Now full of light.

If you endure
It will go on forever.
It will bring you to
A distant place.

Where God will meet you face to face.
So, be strong and go on.
Sing a new song.
God has loved you for so long.

Fault

I will admit my fault
But you would not.
I can see where things went wrong;
You stayed there too long,
Thinking that you were strong.
All I can say is, so long.
So long; admit you were wrong

Frost

Frost last night
When the day was out of sight.
The sun disappeared,
The night leered.

Summer is not yet here.
This is what every flower feared,
Looking for an early Spring.
The birds spread their wings.

Why does the gloom of Winter hang?
When every bird sang

A chirpy little song.
I have waited so long.

Why do I feel so low,
Just when the flowers start to grow?
The hard long winter with its snow
Took its toll I know.
Still I wait every day.
Will this gloom go away?

Will the birds sing
And bring everything?
Will my heart jump for joy,
Or will I sit here and sigh.
Maybe even cry?
But still I ask why.

Just as the sun beams from the sky
And out abroad
I watch people die.
They are fighting for freedom.
Yes, all day I see them.

The whole world has lost its way.
I see this more every day.
I still keep in touch
With those I love so much.

Some are out of touch.
But still the seasons change.
My life to rearrange.

God has given us so much.
He is not out of touch.
He loves us so much.

He hears the birds sing,
Knows that now it's Spring,
Watches the flowers grow,
Row by row.

He died on the cross
For you and me
To set us all free.
That's why I linger here so long,
Otherwise I would be long gone.

The world has no hold on me.
That's the Eternal Key.
I await my destiny.
Trust God all the way.

That's all you can do each day.
The frost will melt away
One sweet sunny day.

The gloom will disappear
And leave room
For joy soon.

The flowers will grow
row by row.
The birds will sing.
Along will come a lovely Spring.

God releases His love and every good thing.
That's what He has done all the time.
Even in gloom you will find
He reaches out to you all the time.

You have to believe,
Not get deceived
And forget to receive
All He has for you
With a love so humble and true.

That's all

I drowned all my sorrows,
Made no plans for all my tomorrows.
Looked through glassy eyes,
Saw no blue skies.

Saw all my dreams
And all my hopes.
Watched them elope.
All my emotion
Deep- deep as the ocean,
Still I can't find,
As I leave them all behind.

They may have left their mark
As I waited in the dark.
For you have given me one word.
You always said I was no good.
All through the years I reached out.
You responded with a shout,
For you were letting me go.
I thought you were friend but you were foe.
You never did relent.
After all the years we spent,
You were hell bent,
Didn't want our Saviour who was sent.
To save your soul
Was His goal.

I helped you through the years,
Putting up with all your fears.
Thought you would see it in the end.
You I tried to defend.

Now you are all alone,
Except for your four-legged friends
And the small hut that you share.
I wouldn't go there, I wouldn't dare.

You never came to your senses,
Putting up all those fences.
I would say you lost the plot,
Couldn't handle all you got.
You gave the children's food to
The dogs.

The dark lady was your downfall.
I tried to tell you all,
But you wouldn't take the call.

Now you must live
And learn to forgive.
Jesus still will give
You salvation, and you will live
Eternally if you will
Acknowledge Him, for your light is dim
Without Him.
Remember this call or you will fall.
That's all.

Riverside

Gentle unused riverside,
With a glowing tide
That riffles through the night,
Until God's holy daylight
Unchanged for many years,
Drifting on without any fears
Along its way home,
Riffling on all alone.
The sunlight softly glows
and on the river flows;
It washes the stones
With its soft and gentle tones.
It's a sight merely to be seen,
And around its pastures, every green.
I take time to stop and take in its ware,
In a world that is fast, and greatly unfair;
But the river never stops to waste time,
On and on it goes; it toes the line.
And I can't think why
As I bid this gentle river goodbye,
Only God knows why.

Osama Bin Laden

Osama Bin Laden,
Where were you heading?
You blew up the towers,
Kept us on edge all these hours.

You were trailed far and wide:
Where did you hide?
What was your problem?
You sent many hobbling.

What was your decision?
What was your direction?
You seemed to have a master plan,
Then you took off and ran.

You left a lot of despair,
Showed us that you didn't care,
Treated so many unfair.

Back stage we waited
While you celebrated;
You thought you had it all,
Until Obama made that call,
Living behind the high wall
In Pakistani high,
Beneath a deadly sky.

Someone gave away the game,
Bring to an end your fame.

You had a darkened mind;
There are many more of this kind.
All you wanted to do was kill
And man to do your will.

Do you know that there's a God above
Who taught us how to love?
Have you ever heard the gospel preached,
Or was it out of your reach?
What were you trying to teach?
You were out of touch,
Why hate so much?

Now it's far too late
For you, at any rate.

All our leaders now agree
It wasn't safe to leave you free.
God said thou shalt not kill,
But you got shot by man's will
As you hid behind the hill.

A dangerous man on the run,
Everything was settled with the gun:
Now you are no longer on the run.

I cannot say that I agree,
But you were dangerous, don't you see?
Killing you was a shocking thing to do;
It's not an eye for an eye
Or a tooth for a tooth;
Man has reached the roof,
And in him came out the brute.
It's easy to shoot.

To re-educate the man
would be best,
Then he could stand with the rest.
Only God knows best.

10 Downing Street

The Labour had to fleet,
The victory for the Tories was sweet
With the government's two seats.

They say, "Pay all the overheads,
By a better government be led.
We will sort the nation's health."
The pinch by all will be felt;
Who will store up the wealth?

This man wanted power,
Can he hold on to the hour?
We have put a lot of trust,
Fight for us he must.

Stop the liquor louts;
Can you hear the shouts?
They end up in A & E,
Who will pay the fee?

Drink and drugs
Wind up the thugs,
Then they fall out
When full of stout.

They waste police time
As they usually get a fine:
Doesn't stop them next time.
What are they trying to say
As they fall around every day?

HANDS ACROSS THE OCEAN

10 DOWNING STREET
LONDON SW1A 2AA
www.number10.gov.uk

From the Direct Communications Unit   29 April 2013

Ms Bridget White

Bristol
BS4

Dear Ms White

I am writing on behalf of the Prime Minister to thank you for your recent correspondence.

Yours sincerely

Correspondence Officer

These are our youth
Giving us all the boot;
Is it a cry
as it's us they defy?

What are they trying to say,
Carrying on this way?
Did you take away God?
Make them carry a heavy load?

No church
Left them in the lurch;
Where do they get their education?
Keep them out of this situation.

Only God knows what happens
When He goes out of their lives.

Then out come the knives
And destroyed are their lives.

Bring GOD back
Before you get the sack.

9/11 USA — Echoes of Broken Glass

Jesus said "Love one another,"
Then the world will not be blown asunder.
The flames burnt high
Over a darkened sky;
The awful news reached our ears,
Bringing with it all our fears.

These, the people we trusted?
Now all these tears;
Madness hit our world that day
In such a dreadful way.

Why did you do this to us?
You came in among us
And we had trust.
You built your mosques,
Opened your shops,
Served goods to the people.

We shared everything with you;
In return this is what you do.
Those twin towers
Were built so high,
Not meant for all those
People to die.

9/11, a dark day
for the USA;
The world watched on,
It's not ok,
The world put you
On trial;
God you are defying

And He will be your final judge,
And bring you to book
For the innocent lives you took.

God will have the final say
For the lives you took
That day:
Echoes of broken glass.

You came in to work among us,
Then through the sky
You flung us.
The day became known
As 9/11.
How I hope they believed in
God and heaven.

Firemen lost their lives too,
When they went in two by two;
They were brave men who
Wouldn't betray
Humanity like YOU did that day.

The twin towers stood up high;
You desired to blow them
Through the sky.
You gave no thought
About the priceless lives,
The dear husbands and wives
And the parents who
Lost their lives,
Or the poor kin left behind.

This was an act
So unkind.

Only God's love will help,
You'll find.

A few months before 9/11 which shocked the whole world, I had a dream. I saw some very tall buildings burning down. A voice said, "All the merchandise is in these buildings, but unless the Lord builds, you labour in vain." I felt the place shake. I told many people in advance. The day after the dream I drew the three buildings and the other details in the picture you see here.

Amy

Amy, you lost your way,
The drugs won today;
You had talent, riches and fame,
Drugs and drink was your game,
Your mind and body so abused
By all the drugs you used.
You had all that money could buy:
Now you are dead. Why?

You still had all your life to live,
And so much more to give;
I heard there were a few,
One of God's people who knew.
You covered your body in tattoos,
Shows how little you knew;
You had all, you had nothing,
All faded by the drugs you had gotten.
We watched, we hoped, we prayed
You wouldn't go this way.
What was your gripe
With this life?

If talent, looks and money are not enough,
And your life was still tough,
Did you have a weak will?
If so, the drugs will surely kill.
How much more must we endure?
Is there no cure?
As we watch our young wiped away
From a system in decay,

To your family and friends
I bid adieu
To the lovely girl
We all knew.
Please, God, help our young,
Put them in the next song.
Bye-bye, Amy.

Tsunami

For what we seen today
We have to pray;
It's no good,
There came a big flood.
Please, God, help the
People of Japan,
Lend them a hand
For they are crying out
In pain,
Their emotions in wane.
These people have been broken
And wildly awoken;
They are left empty handed,
Poverty has landed.
The young and the old
Are out in the cold.
Please, God, bring
Them back into the fold.
I reach up a holy hand
And pray that they land
Back on their feet,
These people gentle and meek;
Every day I pray,
In our heart they stay.
I send an urgent prayer
To God up there,
"Look down on the lost towns,
These souls be saved
Beneath
The waves.
O God, remember their plight
As they went without a fight
To face their darkest night.

First they were shaken,
Left forsaken;
Some never did waken
But returned to their Maker
Before they had time
To bid goodbye to those left behind.

Immigration

Joanna and Noel – two of my children

They say our land has been taken over
By men who come in through Dover;
Some men tried to come in by plane,
They sent them home again.
Some assembled in the border of France,
Waiting to see England at a glance.

Is it a land waiting with the dole
Where the pound will really roll?
There are thousands already here,
and just as many waiting over there.

Some come in on the back of a wagon:
The coast guards are lagging.
England is the place to be,
There you can roam free;
They have a better chance
If they can get over to France.

They may not have an English passport,
But the young ladies they have come to court;
There they will settle down
Under the English Crown.
Of course, it will never be home,
To get here they had to roam;
Their own country didn't provide,
In fact, some have come here to hide:
Like the sea-weed they came in with the tide.

God is always on their side, for them He will provide.
He loves the Man, Women and Child
Who are hungry and have to hide;
He knows about immigration
On every occasion.

Volcano

The dust settles over England,
There are no planes flying overhead:
Only birds flying instead.
A volcano has erupted,
All the planes flying disrupted.

The heaven above is clear,
Not a cloud there to see;
We are living in the end times I fear
When Jesus' return is near.
Man must lay down every plan;
On his feet must land.
When everything in this world doesn't work,
The enemy is on the lurk.

We are here but for a while,
And we must walk on through every dreary mile.
Knowing Jesus we can smile,
He knows what we are going through;
He loves me and you,
And when the dust settles
Over England's shores
And God closes all the doors,
Will we bend a knee before Him?

See that we are out on a limb,
Can we see how fragile we are?
Not to go too far, like this,
Raging with our fist,
Cursing and shouting:
God is being outed.

We must take time to bend a knee,
Otherwise we will never be free

To serve a Saviour that
Died for you and me.

Repent from every wrong,
Come out now, don't take long,
Every minute is precious in His sight.
You know He is always right;
Don't turn your back,
Walk into the dark night:
Of the whole world, Jesus is The Light.

Why would you not listen and obey?
Living life your own way is not ok,
It only leads to hell,
And there, throughout eternity you will dwell,
In a burning fire
That no man should desire.

Where are all your senses?
No good putting up all these fences,
They will not shelter you
Because there is very little that you can do.
When you are faced with God,
You are through.
He wants to be your living Saviour,
But because of your bad behaviour
He has now become your Judge,
And unless you repent
To hell you will be sent.

Can't you see
It's now down to you?
Jesus died on the Cross,
He saw it through,
Died for me and you.

Throughout all Eternity we can go free,
Unless of course you will not bend the knee.
Repent, turn to Him and be free,
He has done all He can for you.

Now, what will you do?
There is no middle ground,
Guilty you will be found
If you don't turn around.

There is only heaven and hell:
Throughout Eternity, where will you dwell?
The heart is deceitful above all,
And beyond cure.
Look at God's Word
And become a doer;
This is your only chance:
Bend the knee and be free.

God has made all the provision,
Don't be kept out by all your decisions;
You cannot trust your own heart,
It will keep you and Jesus apart.

Read God's Word,
Have faith it's true;
All that's in there do, do, do.
Nowhere else will you find
What is truly true.

Come on in, the door is open to you.
Jesus is really true,
He really died for you;
You will be saved if you do
From the raging fire of hell.

March 2011

2011. Such a year of unrest,
Everyone is put to the test;
There are wars breaking out
Here, there and everywhere.
All foreign fields,
No crop do they yield.

All are up in arms
Ringing out great alarms,
Breaking news
Of such abuse,
Many are losing their lives.
Who could survive?

We watch it on the news,
All seem to be confused;
They kick up a big fight,
Fighting for their right.

Who could heed
The man who takes the lead,
If he is a known controller
And not a counsellor?

When the people sigh and die,
We ask why, why, why?
When will men find peace?
The Earth is only ours on lease.

One day God will require our past,
On Him all our sin was cast:
He is the First and He is the Last.

All the fighting that we do,
We are only passing through.

Pray for peace for all;
Please, God, hear that call,
Save them all.

William and Kate's Wedding Date

Prince William and Kate
Have settled their wedding date.
It's April twenty eleven,
A match made in heaven.
They make a fine pair;
She's dark, he's fair.
They have their whole lives ahead,
Now they will soon be wed.
They met long ago;
They love each other so.

Now they are making all their plans
Which will include prams.
They will live a life of bliss
With all of this.
As they tie the knot,
See what God has got.
A plan they will both endure,
Stay together for sure.

He will be the King,
She will be the Queen;
They will both be seen,
They will work together keen.
They will have great times of all kinds.
They will lift up Britain,
All will be smitten;
On England's throne they will be sitting
At a time when changes will come
And the young will be on the run.

By God's grace they will run the race,
Not close the gate on their true faith.
Life for them will be full

And never dull.
They will endeavour to be very clever,
Keep themselves together:
United they will stand
Right through to the end,
Their country by God's grace to defend.

All people will love them;
See what a gem, in England's Crown,
The spark will be found
Whenever they are around.

Bridget White

BUCKINGHAM PALACE

21st March, 2013

Dear Miss White,

    The Queen has asked me to thank you for your poem which you composed for Her Majesty.

    Your words of support for The Queen are most appreciated, and I am enclosing a message from Her Majesty in response to your kind thoughts in on the recent celebrations for The Queen's Diamond Jubilee.

                  Yours sincerely,

                    Miss Jennie Vine
      Deputy to the Senior Correspondence Officer

Miss Bridget White.

Our Queen

You are our Queen,
All over the world you have been,
And on every TV screen.

You really do have it all.
Being Queen was your life's call;
You wear the crown,
Have your face on every pound.

Everyone has a look-in;
You brought up our future King,
Married a man who speaks his mind,
You walk in front, he walks behind.

Buckingham Palace is your home,
As a Queen, you walk alone
On England's throne.
On Christmas TV seen in every home.

You always wear a smile
As you walk mile for mile;
You are not ashamed to follow Jesus:
God, this pleases.
Stay where you are,
You can still go far.

Chains

The cruel chains of injustice
Had me anchored to its shores,
The condemnation was all loaded
on board.

My destination, Oh I don't know where;
My heart was overflowing with bitterness,
The cruel chains of injustice had entangled
my heart.

The deep hatred that I felt
Was an added distress,
Packed with cases of loneliness,
Locked inside any hope of happiness.

Only the outer shell of emptiness,
The cruel chains of injustice,
The burden too much for me to bear:
O God, tell me that You care.

Help me to forgive, to live,
He hurt me to the core;
Help me to forgive,
My life to You I give.

Jesus was nailed to the cross,
He picked up all my loss;
Now I am anchored
To this great cause,
I have taken His word on board.

He will give me His justice,
He will forgive my sins;
I am made up for life,
Handed over all the strife.

Time

You cannot catch it,
It moves so fast;
At times it seems so slow
When you have nowhere to go.

When you have time on your
Hands you are rich;
Money cannot buy time,
Nor can you hold it back.

It belongs to no man
But everyone has it;
You can waste it,
Run out of it.

They say time is money,
Time waits for no man,
But time is a precious thing;
It's a twenty-four hour cheque
That you can spend as you wish.

You can be early or late with time;
Time holds a day and a date,
But only God holds time:
You cannot tell time to wait.

If you squander it, you will be late;
Time does not heal: it only passes.
Look at the clock with your glasses,
You cannot catch time,
You cannot pass it by.

Sometimes it seems to fly.
When it runs out, you die.

God made time; He knows about it,
We can't get by without it.

We try to keep up with it,
We are ruled by it;
Time, time, time – that's fine,
But I am fed up keeping it,
Only to discover it has passed on by.

I am ahead of time, some say.
Who are you fooling?
Time is the master,
It rules over you.

You run out of it,
It has no respect for anyone,
It goes on regardless;
You cannot see it or feel it,
But it always overtakes you.

It's like the Liffey flowing on,
It burst its banks, then it's gone;
Time waits for no man,
Man is in fear of it.

Hours hold it;
We think: I do not like it,
Especially when I am behind;
It's a force,
Let God deal with it.

Mountain High

Mountain high my soul do lie,
Because of things in my past do I sigh,
And unlike a bird I cannot fly:
Upon my word I will not die.

I promise to look back no more
To that distant shore,
And it will rest on my heart no more:
It has tried to eat me to the core
And has brought along companions galore.
It hangs over me night and day
and refuses to go away.

Mountain high my soul do lie,
Because of things in my past do I sigh,
And unlike a bird I cannot fly:
No, I am not lost but found.

No, I am not on the mountain,
But my feet have found the ground;
I promise to look back no more
To that distant shore
Where I got wounded before
And where enemies were at me galore,
It no longer hangs over me night and day,
And through Jesus I will tell it to go away:
Him it must obey.

Mountain high my enemies do lie,
And unlike a bird they cannot fly,
And upon my word I will not die,
Because from the cross I heard my Saviour's cry.

My Steps Are Built on Heartache

My steps are built on heartache,
To discover a world full of fake;
I make a collection of all the rejection
That hangs in the galleries of what was once my home.

My steps are built on faith, hope and love,
Like petals that are falling from above,
Crowning my every step, even where I have slept;
It does not matter what you think because I have
Made the all important link.

It may be too much for you to comprehend,
By the way, it's not ever meant to offend,
Or to know how the intellect think:
Maybe you can't even make the link.

Don't worry, maybe you begin to think
My steps are built on victory all the time,
Because I have learned to walk the line.
My education came through the lowly kind,
Not pretending to be someone I am not is fine.

My steps are built on marble
When most have lost theirs;
I go on and on without any fears,
I have hope all my years.

I hold the very keys that open every door,
I go even higher, when others go lower;
It's not for me to look down on the very poor,
Some have even slept on the floor.

When the last will be first,
The water of their thirst
Will be fed
And not misled.

They will not be rejected or cast out
By those who hold such clout;
But God will bring them in,
They shall not be kept out.

So fix your eyes upon Jesus,
And the things of this world
Will go strangely dim
In the light of His wonderful love.

Japan, Japan, Japan

O Japan, Japan,
The water and the debris,
Oh how it ran.
The earthquake
Destroyed all in its wake
As the earth did shake.

Many souls were lost,
For living on the earthquake's crust.
One of the biggest ever,
With them we would like to sever.

As the earthquake shook,
The river burst:
We could only look on in despair,
Feel how we care,
Watching those poor people over there;
For I cannot comprehend
How it will end.

O God, what can we do?
If only, in advance we knew,
Now we can only hope and pray
Help will come to them today,
To build up their lives another way.
Things will never be the same.
No one is to blame:
It's a vast land all the same.

Little by little they will build up again,
But people lost, what a cost,
Gone forever.
Have mercy, dear God.
It only goes to show
When life is going slow
In a natural kind of flow,

You never can see what's to be,
Or how long we will live here,
Be in God's tender-loving care.
Every day make sure to stay there.
For in the end, that's all we have,
Where the tsunami rivers flow,
Or not, is all we've got.

Pray for Japan, for these people,
For their land:

Pray every day.
God's way be done

Japan, Japan, Japan,
What is your future plan?
You have taken such a shake,
Now you must be awake.
The water had such a force,
Took everything in its course.
While many were gone to their sleep,
Many more are left to weep.
Is the world reaching its end?
Please, God, we ask You to defend.

Japan, Japan, Japan's people,
I say a silent prayer
For all them over there.
I know that your suffering is so deep and in my heart I silently weep.
I pray God for you to keep,
To heal you, for those who sleep,
To know that this is not the end.

For Jesus will soon return;
In His love He will yearn for His people to return
As His saving grace
lights up every face.
As the world shakes upside down,
Don't forget it's Jesus who won the crown.
Do not be alarmed,
You are safe in HIS ARMS;
He has a plan that will outrun man.
Come now, and take His call:
This is to All.

War, War, War

The war in Afghanistan,
It's fought mainly by Man;
Among the dusty hills they die,
Their blood spills – all cry.

Every day I pray it stops,
And the killing drops;
We hear on the daily news
All the human abuse.

Who do we blame?
For all those flying out by plane,
Have they thought
Why this war is fought?

Why do so many die,
Flying aircraft through the sky?
They have lots of ammunition:
What's their ambition?

What is their final goal,
When people are dying out cold?
It's a dusty no man's land
They are trying to defend.

Lots of our young soldiers have died,
Lots of poor people have cried;
We despair: all war is unfair,
Our young are dying.

God is crying,
Love can conquer all;
Why die and fall

In a distant land
Called Afghanistan?
Let these people alone
To build their own country and home.

Some have been hostile,
Came to our country to defile;
By this we cannot judge them all
But work together to end the war
So that God's love can conquer all.

A burn victim

I Would Rather

The last few weeks of 2010
Will never be here again;
The snow fell fast and deep
All while we were asleep.

This has been a fast year
Although I have just moved in here
There are many things I cannot afford,
Rubbish in all my bags I hoard,
As I have sat for the past ten years
Leaving behind all my fears.

Now I must move on,
Saying to the past, so long, be gone.
Don't crop up in my dreams
For I want to forget, it seems.
There are many faces, places I want to forget,
That's if I am let.

It's not that I don't care,
It's better to leave them all there;
There's a lot to be said for moving on.
Let there be a new song.

The dawn breaks forth once a day,
Then we can all have our say.
All our memories we can keep,
They will pop up now and then in our sleep:
Sometimes with a new spin,
We can't always win.

What can make a winner out of one man
Can make a loser out of another;
You might say, why bother?
But when all's said and done,
I would rather.

Give Up Smoking

Give up smoking,
Give up joking,
Give up your money,
Come on now, sonny,
You know it makes sense:
Stop sitting on the fence.
Smoking does kill:
Is that your will?

You are doing harm:
Does that set off the alarm?
Many people die;
Those left behind cry.
You are not only hurting yourself,
Think of those left on the shelf.
I plead with you today:
From fags, stay away.
God will help you
If you do,
So be strong
And say, "So long."

Yes, bid them adieu;
Please, will you?
Please do.
I am asking you,
Don't harm yourself,
Leave them on the shelf.
Be strong, say No,
Then your money will grow,
Your health will soar,
Your body will be glad
That sense at last you had.

The will to do what's right,
And put that ugly fag to flight,
Out of sight,
Never to return
Or yearn for the ugly weed
That makes so many mourn.
God loves you,
Do you love you?

Memories

I travelled through my memories
Walking through the evening breeze,
And above the wind blowing through the trees.
Memories long forgotten,
The sun getting hotter,
The pebbles beneath my feet,
My tired feet to greet.

The places, the races and the faces
Of long forgotten places
Return to my mind:
Those I have left behind.

As the stars come out above
My heart is filled with love
for those I once knew;
My pains are many, not few,
For deep within my memory
Until a trigger came
And pressed the button –
Finished was the game
That kept my emotions lame.

And out came all the pain.
I had to know once again
Right there in the evening breeze;
Out fell all the keys
That had locked up all these
Memories I cannot hide,
That come flooding in like the tide.

The sun has gone to set,
My memories won't let
Me forget.

Just like the tide
And the emotions I cannot hide.

I must sit here and
Let the emotions flow
For there's nowhere that I can go.

I talk to God
And let Him know;
He meets me right
Here on this road,
Said "Let down your load."

He pours down His love and rest,
My memories are
Put to flight.
Gone is my darkest night:
In God's Holy Light.

2013

2013 hasn't yet been;
They said the world
Would end this year:
It's God they should fear.

He has all authority here;
Just bend the knee
Then you will see
He wrote the book
Of Revelation.

This is where you should station;
Find out what it says,
All about the end days
When the enemies
Come to attack.

No good looking back,
We win in the end;
Now make your choices.
Do think twice,
Whose side will you take?
Be true or fake,
Don't refuse
And lose.
Jesus paid the price.

2013 is here,
It's there,
It's everywhere.
The world didn't end,
To God, thanks I send,
I still want to live

To God to give
My everything.

Yes, ever sing;
I would like to sing in tune.
Maybe I will soon.
There's not many
Birds around.
This I have found;
Some have fallen
From the sky –
Can no longer fly,
So they drop down and die.
I wonder why.

The Summer Rose

I am resting in the sweet repose,
And through the window
The scent of the summer rose;
My heart broken in a hundred pieces,
The hurt and pain releases;
Through the many ups and downs,
The feeling of being lost, God I found.

I had not been on the right road,
I couldn't carry my load,
I had picked up things that were not mine.
Myself, among the tatters I could not find;
I was lost in a maze of hurt and shame,
And I looked for others to blame.
Surely, wherever I leave it, it will be all the same.

Then God said to me, "Don't blame the lame.
Give to me your pain and shame;
Because I sent my Son to die for you
Don't let that be in vain.
He will carry all your pain;
Forgive all your sin and shame,
For there's no more that I can do
For mankind like you."

I am resting on sweet repose,
The smell of the late summer rose;
God is close to the broken- hearted,
From them He will never be departed.
Through the years of ups and downs
You will know it's God you found.

He wants you on the straight and narrow;
Your troubles along with you, He will carry,

Then He will guide you through them all.
Never again will you be lost or fall:
On the cross of Calvary he paid the cost,
Jesus
(He is the truth, the way, the life.)

Winter Winds

When winter winds blow
And there is no trace of snow,
And the trees are all bare,
Does nature no longer care?

There is a cloud hanging over the sky,
Between winter and summer there is no tie,
But division.
From winter to summer, it takes a decision.

When the leaves fall,
And then winter has come to call,
And each sit around the fire,
And work for tomorrow is put out on hire,
Is it fair?
Does nature no longer care?

Winter winds are unkind,
Summer is much better I find.

Time Holds No Place

Time holds no place for us;
We may stand on the shore,
But together we would be wrong to the core.
I must forget you exist,
Your charms I must resist;
It's better to walk away
Than to get it wrong and stay.
You mean a lot to me,
But it's better if you're free;
To my happiness you hold the key,
And I hold the key to set you free.
You go left and I go right,
And together for our freedom we must fight;
What's wrong can't be right.

Just a dream away,
You're like a faded picture,
In my mind a long lost fixture;
But now and then
I pick you up again,
And to my memory
A shock you send.
I look at your face
And on this I rest my case.

It was this that made me really care,
Now you are gone it's unfair;
So I can't turn back the clock.
In my life you would
Have been a steady rock,
But you are only a faded picture,
In my mind, a long lost fixture:
Lost in time.

Crying in the Wilderness

Come on, boy,
Get up, don't die,
God's heard your cry.

Lying so low,
Nowhere to go;
This muddy street,
Your tired feet.

Where is your hope?
Don't let it elope;
Come on, boy,
God's heard your cry.

What made you give up?
Come on, stop,
Don't lie so low,
There is somewhere to go.

Come on, boy,
Don't live a lie;
God loves you more
With gifts in store.

Come on, boy.
Don't die;
Get your hope,
Give up dope.

The Moon Looked On

The moon looked on
When the sun was gone,
The stars lit up a darkened night
When the sun was out of sight,
At the break of dawn
When the stars and moon were gone,
A new day came to call.

The trees were white with frost,
And to us the summer was lost.
The winter had come to call,
Leaving behind the autumn fall.

Old memories now tap on my thoughts,
Bidding me once again to look in
At all my faraway kin.
The pain as I look through
The faded pane,
At the green grass that
Was fading fast,
Under the summer sun.

The children playing outside,
Playing seek and hide;
We didn't have much to eat,
Although the fields had barley and wheat.

This was a land that once had a famine:
No lakes full of cod, hake and salmon.
The hearts of many growing cold,
They sold our goods abroad.
We had nothing, they had gold;
We all had to emigrate

Before it was too late.
The RC Church from Rome
Had taken hold.
The lock was not only locked
But bolted.
They told us what to do,
We thought best they knew.
They brought their own kind of law;
We heard about it, but never saw.
They told us, save your pennies
For far-off lands.

We carried our free milk home
In cans.
"Help the poor," they preached,
How come us they couldn't reach?
Keep the home fires burning,
To the mission fields go a-running.

Help begins at home,
Then you couldn't afford to roam;
We had no pay,
Couldn't afford our bread,
Were starved and not fed.

Can you spare a thought
For our survival we fought?

Come on Rome, couldn't you help?
We knocked on your door,
Asked for a little help or more:
You had plenty in store.
Why send me away
With an empty hand?

> Was it me, or God you did offend?
> After all, God loves the poor:
> You should have known that before.

At Night

I stay wake at night,
Gone is all my delight,
Far away out of sight;
The lonely days rolled along,
Far away was my song,
What was it that went wrong?

If my heart must stay low,
For it was you I love so,
My hurt and pain you never saw,
For I kept my emotion locked in.

I knew I'd lose and never win,
For it was always your sin
To break my heart
Before I had time to start.

Could you see my wrath
Blocking up all my path?
For tonight my heart is still,
Of pain I have had my fill,
It's all about doing God's will.

For if you follow your own way
You will surely go astray
And a trap the enemy will lay.

So take instruction,
Stop kicking up ruction,
The enemy will make up concoction.

For there is a plumb-line
If you look hard enough you will find;
Go on ahead, don't look behind.

God has all the answers,
No good taking all the chances,
For I lived in your shadow;
Listen to God I'd rather,
Because you only made me sadder;
I looked after child;
You went out wild.

I tried to make you see
How wrong you could be;
You could have taken a better way,
Then the child would stay.

All you do is drink and drug,
Be a street-tough;
You wouldn't listen,
I blew the whistle.

What else could I do
But grass on you?
You left me no choice,
For chances I gave you twice.

You never faced
But ran in haste,
You want to party all the time;
Lose your life, you'll find
You will not pick up the pieces
Or I ran out the crises.

You are surely letting us all down,
On your father's forehead a frown;
You rob all around,
Never left them a pound,
You play all around.

People's emotions
Bring them to ground:
No love in you to be found.

The Fall-Away

The hearts of many grow cold,
Despair for the young and old;
There will be a great fall away,
So the Bible says.

We are in perilous times,
No one kind,
(Jesus told us so);
His love to us will flow
Wherever we go.

Don't be deceived,
In Him believe;
He knows it all,
Hear and obey His call.

Don't be part of the great fall;
He has promised us,
In Him we can trust
That He is coming back.

Gone will be all the lack,
He will give us an eternal home,
No more will we need to roam;
Our Saviour is our great love,
It's that that He pours
Down from above.

We were no good,
Through Him we can live,
His righteousness He will give;
To you He will be true,
So repent, He was sent
To save you.

In Vain

Man's shattered plans deceive,
It starts with unbelief
In God above so high
Whom they all deny
To their own cost.
They remain lost
And won't accept the Cross;

If only they could see,
Then they would be free,
Not just now, but eternally.
To them it is all free,
Jesus paid the price for you and me,
There He lost his life.
Sin in this world was rife,
Our destiny, hell for life,
Except Jesus paid the price
With His whole life.

So why would you deny,
Live a life full of lies?
Can't you hear His cries?
All you have to do is follow,
Leave behind this life, so hollow.
Jesus said "Follow me,
Then you'll be free."
There is no middle ground,

You will remain lost not found
If you don't take heed
And take Jesus' lead.
There is nothing in this world, I can promise you,
If you don't take this way, you will rue;

One day it will be too late
To wipe clean that slate:
You will have sealed your own fate.

God has made the provision
For your living;
All this to you He has given,
Don't give it all away,
Walk this way today.

It's a gift
Which will uplift;
Do not despise an eternal paradise,
Do not run and hide
Because Jesus died
So that you could live
Eternally free.
Amen.

Autumn

In Autumn the leaves are falling,
Then I will come a-calling
To take you to my paradise,
And only then you will realise
Life is worth living
When you are giving.
There will be no deceiving
Or leaving.
Faithful love is what God requires,
The old ways must expire;
In the Spring
you will love everything,
The butterflies will all be free
To fly on their wings;
Your every emotion
Will cross the ocean,
There will be no hesitation
On this occasion.
All your pain will fade away
On this your special day;
Every little flower
Has the power
To touch your soul.
God has a reason
For this season,
You deserve all the best:
God will do the rest.
Then in the summer of your life
God will give you a wife;
Go now and live your life
For God has made a pathway
In which you walk each day.
All your dreams are on their way.

Rest My Case

Cameron got into 10, Downing Street,
Now he has landed on his feet;
He has a country to run
That's been drunk and full of fun.
The street kids been having
The time of their lives,
Running wild with the drugs and knives;
The drug hostels full to the brim,
Oh yes our land has gone very dim.

The government pays for their addictions,
While they drug up and kick up ructions.

Oh sure, they have left home,
To stand on their feet alone.
But it's the government
Who supports their lifestyle;
Lots of them are dying all the while.
Mick Jagger saw a black door
And he wanted to paint it red,
Ever since, the kids have been misled,
Gave the kids bad tips.
The days of Rock 'n' Roll
Our youth have stole;
They all thought
They had something great,
But look at them now, what a state.

But Mr Cameron is a clean-cut man,
The youngest Prime minister to stand;
He has three children of his own,
Can he bring the truth home
To those street-kids out there all alone?
Can he help the parents to take over,
Help the kids get sober?

He is sitting in 10, Downing Street,
Got all this at his feet.
Is he going to be able to see
How to get them free?
He has always had
The best of everything:
Can he get in this ring,
Take on a land that is on its knees?
Does he hold the keys?

We also have a Credit Crunch.
We're in trouble, what a bunch.
No, Cameron has a right-hand man,
Nick Clegg is his name:
For this fight, is he game?
Will they work together well?
God has a plan
To bring down man;
A leader should acknowledge
There is Someone greater than him
Whose light is not dim.

Cameron will not succeed
If he does not heed;
Like all the others he will
Have regrets, frets,
He will lose the plot
Before his baby's out of the cot.
It's only God's plans
That will succeed;
Mr Cameron, take heed.

Clegg doesn't believe,
He has tricks up his sleeve,
Thinks God doesn't exist,

Put up his prayer fists.
But in the end, he will
Not defend righteousness
When he is put to the test
He will face,
Like all the rest.
Without God, you are all lost,
To your own cost
If you deny the Cross.

Bella, Dear

Hello Miss Bella, Bella Dear,
How nice to meet you here;
I can see your hair has grown long,
And in your heart a new song.
You go to school every day,
And that's really ok,
You enjoy all things
Even when the little bird sings.
You like to dress up,
There's nowhere to stop
When it comes to dressing up.
You are at the top,
You have two eyes like a dove,
Sending out true love,
You are the neatest person I know,
Always helping me when I am low.
I wish you well
Wherever you go,

Only God can know
How we all love
You so xxx.
You will be blessed
As your family have invest,
With interest,
All their best.
You will do the rest.
So here is a little poem,
Wherever you roam.
Always keep it
At home:
From your grandmother
Far across the foam.

Barack Obama

The first black man to rule
America's land;
This man plays his cards
Close to his chest,
He may or may not be a step
Above the rest.
As of yet he has not
Been put to the test.

Is he a God believer
Or a high class deceiver?
Jesus said, "It's by the fruit they bear
That you will see what's in their care."
He goes to a lot of rounds,
Travels all the towns;
If you listen to what he say,
He doesn't give a lot away.
Surely sooner or later, we will see
What's on this tree.
What has he got to hide?
It will all come in like the tide;
Is it written in his eyes?
He has a soft spot for the Arab guys.
Is it their oil that may last
Only a while?
When all's said and done
On the case of Bin Laden
He won.

They say he is of Irish descent,
His family out of Ireland went;
When times were hard
They played their last card,

They landed on American shore.
Now in this generation they did score,
And can now claim
He belongs to Ireland just the same.

Does he acknowledge the Cross?
To me he looks quite lost.
It's not the colour of his skin,
Nor the descent of his kin,
But in the end it could be his sin
Because if he doesn't depart
From it, God won't let him in.

So bend the knee,
That's the key,
Don't be proud
Or shout out loud.
He may seem at the top
of his game,
But without God this man is lame.
That's all I have got to say,
So together we all pray:
God, please save this man today.

Epilogue

I met Bridget when we were asked to run a Christian café with five others. A few weeks in, a homeless man came in. Bridget gave him free food. Word got around and very soon lots of homeless came in, the paying customers dropped off and The Shepherd's Tent became a drop-in. That is Bridget.

The two of us ran it for four years with a little help. Then we branched out to Street-evangelism. Bridget was led of God to College Green in Bristol centre where hundreds of teenagers – Gothics and others – congregated. We evangelised there for three years and about 1700 were saved. We go around Bristol and people are saved everywhere – fast food restaurants and skate parks et al. Also there have been big harvests in all the neighbouring towns like Bath, Yate and Nailsea. It happens everywhere, glory to God.

We have been on radio, secular and Christian quite a few times, and in Christian newspapers. We have also gone further afield, doing missions to Ireland, Isle of Wight and Bridgend etc.

Bridget is a prophetess. I remember her showing me her drawings of the twin towers burning four months before they did. She was also warning of the Credit Crunch three years before. She is a very godly lady who has a great heart for everyone including the poor, her family, and saving the lost.

Apostle Simon Farris M.A. [Cantab]
Bristol Underground Church

Simon and me at The Shepherd's Tent

Printed in Great Britain
by Amazon